How to

Retire Happier

The Best Travel, RV, Overseas, Snowbird and Retire-in-Place Lifestyles Plus the Best States for Retirement

Ron Stack

How to Retire Happier

The Best Travel, RV, Overseas, Snowbird and Retire-in-Place Lifestyles Plus the Best States for Retirement

First Edition

Copyright © 2015 by Ron Stack

All rights reserved.

Published in the United States of America
Printed in the United States of America
Published by Zeus Press Inc.

ISBN 978-0-9857792-4-5

Disclaimer

Table of Contents

Introduction

Many retirees have spent decades planning for their retirement, financially, but have done little or no planning of what they will actually be doing during those retirement years. If that's you, don't worry. Helping you plan an exciting, adventurous life after working is the purpose of this book. What's that? You don't need a plan because you're "just going to relax at first"? That might be OK, but starting the very next day after you leave work forever, your brain will realize you're not performing the same routines after being cued as you have for decades.

Starting the very first day of your retirement, your brain is going to be on high alert to figure out what is going on. It will be looking for new cues and routines that it can commit to memory so it can form new habits. If you're not careful, you could wake up one day and realize that ten years have gone by and all you've done is watch the weather channel all day, every day. Or worse. Statistically speaking, people who watch more than 2.5 hours of TV a day have a 300% higher chance of "reaching an early expiration date." After a life of working hard, making sacrifices and taking care of your responsibilities, you deserve better than that.

This book will help you put together a plan for your retirement years based around the two most important things required to retire happier and healthier. You can't be happier if you're not healthy, but you're in luck because we're going to make doing healthy things so much fun, it'll become a big part of your life.

You're also going to learn if it's best to continue living where you are now or move somewhere new for retirement. If moving is right for you, you'll learn the *true* best places to retire, and the worst (sorry, Louisiana). In fact, you'll see all the states ranked by overall quality of life, and also what your chances of being happier might be, if you moved to a particular state.

What if you want to move for retirement, but you have family and friends you don't want to move away from? That's covered in the book. What if you're tired of shoveling snow or want to move somewhere warmer? That's covered too.

Are you better suited to a RV lifestyle than you realize? What about full-time RVing? Would RV snowbirding suit you a better?

Should you retire in place? If so, should you downsize, and what is the one giant advantage to doing so that may go away soon? What about buying a vacation home?

Have you ever wondered what the real costs of living overseas are? Are there downsides, or could it be right for you? Can you really retire for less overseas, and is it safe?

Are people who move to states with lower taxes or no personal income tax happier? Should I take up new activities, hobbies or sports? What about becoming healthier and living longer—is there something we should be doing? All are covered in this book.

If you'd like answers to these questions and more, this book is for you. The purpose of the book is help you choose and plan the most adventurous, exciting and healthful retirement lifestyle possible. Ready to retire happier?

Overseas Combo Retirement Lifestyle

What is it? Traveling and living overseas not as a tourist in hotels, but living like a local in fully furnished homes or apartments. You may live in France for three months, then Italy and the Philippines after that. The great thing is, it's possible to travel and experience life and culture in other countries for less than it would cost you to live in the US.

Just about any couple can afford to experience this adventurous lifestyle, even if the only income you'll have is your social security checks. It would more challenging to do as a single traveler on SS alone, but certainly not impossible (why not find another adventurous single to split the cost of an amazing lifestyle?)

Choosing to do this involves very little risk of being

unhappy because you won't be committing long term to a country you know very little about, and you won't be buying any property. You could start by just planning your first three-month trip and then returning home. If it's something you want to continue to do, you can take off on your first trip and not return home until, well, who knows? You could be on your way to an exciting new life with a new country to explore within weeks after you decide to try it out.

How to Get Started

First, if you don't already have one, you'll need a US passport if you're an American citizen. With a US passport you can stay up to three months as a tourist in many countries around the world. This allows you to skip the hassle and expense of getting a resident visa, which would be needed to live in a foreign country for longer periods or full-time.

Next, do some research and decide the first country you want to visit. What many people don't realize is how cheap it can be to live overseas like a local, rather than as a tourist. No, I'm not talking about visiting only the poorest third world countries. You can certainly do that if you like, but you can live like a local in developed western countries more cheaply than in the US if you do it right.

You'll live in a fully furnished apartment or home. You'll buy groceries in the local stores and cook meals at home, eating out as often as you do now. You'll live like a local outside of the tourist trap areas. This will allow you to learn more about the people and culture of the country. You can get up every day and explore by walking, biking and using the cheap but excellent public transportation systems many countries outside the US have. Every day you can set out to explore, experiencing the best your host country offers. For less than the cost of living in the US, you could be sampling French wines at a vineyard instead of sitting on the couch in Cleveland watching that rerun for the sixth time.

Like some of the other lifestyles in this book, this will probably not be something you'll do for your entire retirement. Many people find exploring a new part of the world every few months very intoxicating, even addicting, and have done it for years. If this sounds like something you may want to do, consider doing it right after you retire. While there's nothing to stop you from doing this at any age, it's easier when you're a younger retiree. It'll give something to talk about when you get older and settle into another retirement lifestyle.

Overseas FAQ's

- Yes, you can receive US Social Security payments if you live overseas.
- No, Medicare will not cover you for medical care while overseas in non-US territories.
- Yes, you will need a valid US passport to enter almost any country. Yes, you will need one to get back into the US from overseas.
- Yes, you can travel up to 90 days in many countries with your US passport and a tourist visa from that country.
- Full-time living or remaining in most countries

for more than 90 days often requires much more paperwork, time and money. Often you must become a legal resident. To avoid disappointment, don't underestimate how challenging this might be in some countries.

- Becoming a legal resident of a country outside of the US does not mean you are a citizen of that country, just that you are allowed to reside there.
- Living in another country and becoming a resident there does not mean you lose your US citizenship. You can generally lose your US citizenship only if you deliberately take the required steps to renounce your US Citizenship.
- Yes, health care in many countries overseas today is just as good as, or according to some reputable worldwide health care organizations, better than medical care in the US.

What Country to Visit First

If you're new to overseas travel, choosing a country where English is widely spoken or at least understood can make your first trip more enjoyable. Learning how to become a smart overseas traveler will happen faster when you can communicate with people in the country you're visiting.

You'll become fluent in getting airline tickets, clearing customs and securing comfortable housing in a new country after you do it a few times. When you become comfortable with traveling, you'll know how to easily set up a home in a new country. When you have that down, you may want to kick the adventure up a notch and explore a country where you'll need to learn the language to enjoy the country to its fullest. If you learn a new language, you could choose only countries that speak that language for a while. You may even come to speak it fluently.

While you're living in your first country, you can make plans to visit next one. If you find you really enjoy a country and would like to spend more time than the tourist visa allows, you may be able just to go across the border into the country next door for eight days or so and return on a new tourist visa. Always check with the authorities of the country so you know what is permissible.

About Overseas Housing

Some travelers prefer to book a place for the entire length of their stay before they even leave the US so they know they have a definite place waiting for them. Others book a place only for a couple of days or a week; then they'll look for a place once they're on the ground in that country. The advantage is that many places available for rent won't be listed with rental services, and they may charge lower prices, often allowing you to deal directly with the owner. You'll also be able to see the place and its surroundings in person before you commit. Pictures online can be deceiving.

Some travelers like the certainty of knowing that they already have their home secured for the entire time they'll be there before they even leave the US. Some travelers find they like dealing with and trust a particular rental listing service and always book through them.

Finding Housing Worldwide

There are overseas accommodation options that will fit just about any budget, even free. Couch surfing offers the opportunity to stay with people who open their homes to travelers without charge, just to meet new people and share their culture. This type of accommodation is perhaps best used as a place to stay for a few days or weeks while you look for a longer term place to rent. Your host(s) may be an invaluable help with that task, especially if you don't speak the local language.

Furnished apartments, or flats as they're know in some countries, and homes can be found through many online websites. You'll find a link at the end of this chapter, and at the end of every chapter in this book, to pages on a website that provides videos, more specific details and helpful links. Consider renting something smaller, because if you do it right, you'll be outside exploring, sightseeing and visiting the cafes so you won't be spending much time indoors.

If you're really adventurous, social and want to save money, staying in a hostel may be an option for you. These dorm style and shared room places are popular with backpackers, but are used by boomers now too. Hostels are popular around the world, but have never been big in the US. There are some bad ones, so consider places that have lots of reviews and a positive rating of 85% or higher.

How to Get Started

Apply for a passport if you don't have one, and if

you already have one, make sure it's not about to expire. Make a list of countries that you've always wanted to visit or chose a few from the ones we'll cover shortly. Then check to see if there are any safety alerts or warnings for travel to the countries on your list from the US State Department. You should also consider signing up for their Smart Traveler Enrollment Program or STEP.

Then it's time to look for short term furnished rental availability and pricing for the countries on your list. Keep in mind that when it's winter here in the US, it's summer in the southern hemisphere. After checking availability and pricing, narrow your choices down to one country and check airline fares to make sure they'll fit within your budget.

Then Just Do It

OK, you've chosen the country for your first adventure. You've got your passport in order. You've determined from the US State Department's site that travel to the part of the country you're going to is safe. You've signed up for the US's STEP program and followed the other tips about packing light and making copies of your documents. You've found a few rentals and airfares available in your price range. It's time to just book it!

It's an adventure, so just book it and go. You'll surely learn ways that you can make your next trip even better. My motto? The worst day adventure traveling beats the best day sitting on the couch, depressed from watching hours of daytime TV programming. Next up, countries to visit!

Summary and Tips

- If you're not retired yet, consider pooling vacation time and renting a furnished home or apartment for a one-month vacation as a test.
- If you are retired, consider planning just one three-month trip to see how you like it.
- Most people will do this only for a few years, and then spend the rest of their retirement in a single location in the US (or overseas if they fall in love with certain country).
- Did you take a foreign language while in school or college? Even if you don't think you recall very much of what you learned, you may enjoy choosing a country that speaks that language because you'll pick it up faster.
- If this is a lifestyle that you will be doing for a few years, you may want to sell your home in the US if you own one, especially if you're going to "right size" or relocate, as covered in latter chapters.

For more helpful information go to:

www.BestPlacesToLiveRetire.com

Then click on the overseas resources link. or use the direct web address below.

http://www.bestplacestoliveretire.com/2015/02/best-places-retire-overseas.html

Inexpensive Adventure Overseas

Castles Art Wine and Spectacular Food

Languedoc-Roussillon, the "other" South of France, is a popular region for short-term living in France. It's far cheaper to live in the South West portion of France near the Spanish border. If you have a modest retirement budget, Carcassonne is an attractive option for retiring in France, especially if you think you'd love medieval towns, castles, art, wine, splendid architecture and of course, delicious food.

Carcassonne and its surrounding countryside are full of culture and tradition—and they're breathtaking! You can be at the Mediterranean coast within an hour from Carcassonne. Provence and the Cote d'Azur may be Languedoc-Roussillon's glossy and famous counterpart in the South East along the

Mediterranean, but the Languedoc boasts as much beauty and charm. Its climate is balmy with mild winters. Retirees can live in such places as beautiful Carcassonne at a fraction of the price that it would cost in Provence and less than in the US if done right.

As in the rest of France, you can benefit from one of the best health-care systems in the world. Doctors' visits run about $30 for non-residents. If you become a resident, health-care can be free or at least heavily subsidized by the government.

As for costs, Carcassonne is a very affordable place to live, with rent around $750 per month. If you are buying, house prices are still relatively low in this region. Since Carcassonne is a major tourist area, retirees may like to buy a property with vacation rental potential to augment their income, especially with the airport and airlines offering cheap flights right on the region's doorstep. Toulouse is a much bigger airport with many more flight options. Carcassonne is a tourist mecca that draws people from all over the world, but you can find quiet areas both in town and in the surrounding countryside.

Considering a retired couple's total monthly expenditure, you could live in Carcassonne reasonably with a budget of about $2000 a month—not bad at all for the opportunity to live in a beautiful, stable, modern western county where you don't have to worry about the government's ability to keep the lights on.

Carcassonne itself, with its magnificent ramparts and towers, is one of the incredible historic sites in the Cather country. The old upper town dates from the Middle Ages and was very well restored in the nineteenth century. Still, don't imagine that Carcassonne is only history and old world tradition.

From a distance, Carcassonne can be clearly seen like a fairy tale scene rising from the horizon, drawing visitors to its magical atmosphere. You cannot fail to fall under the charm of Carcassonne. It's a super chance for any retiree to live an inexpensive, but comfortable dream retirement in historical and romantic surroundings.

The town of Carcassonne has everything you would expect in a lively town with cultural venues and shopping facilities. If you prefer walks along the river, there's the quieter side to the city. Imagine balmy evenings strolling in the winding, cobbled streets of the upper town with all the aromas and sounds. Go back in time with the Chateau Comtal within the outer rampart walls.

Or maybe you prefer the countryside or even a mixture of urban and rural. The Carcassonne vicinity offers a variety of stone-built country houses in quaint villages. Fancy a rolling vineyard view from your bedroom window? Sip a glass of local wine while you ponder your blessings at living your retirement years inexpensively, but comfortably in Carcassonne and the Languedoc.

Subtropical Mediterranean Climate

At the time of this writing, Spain's economy is struggling a little more than Europe as a whole. It's difficult to find a job which isn't a drawback for retirees travel living. Public services during the downturn may not be as reliable as those we're accustomed to in the US, or when compared to France; however, the bad economy has kept prices low, making many locations in Spain a bargain in Europe.

Málaga, Spain is the most southerly large town in Europe, located right on the enchanting Mediterranean Sea. Because of its southern Europe location, it enjoys a subtropical Mediterranean climate with some of the warmest winters in Europe. Temperatures during the day are in the low 60's with cool nights.

Málaga is one of the oldest cities in the world and is rich in history. It's also a lively town with beautiful beaches. Tourist flock there during the winter for its warm weather. Many expats from England, Germany and elsewhere live here, so you'll fit right into this historic but cosmopolitan town.

Oviedo is another beautiful town with reasonable prices, and it's considered by some as one of the cleanest towns in Europe. It's a safe place with lots of historic areas to explore downtown, including one of Europe's most impressive cathedrals. The nearby town of Gijón is also very worth considering, especially if you want to be near the beach. Santander too is a beautiful town with friendly people, good prices, and a beach.

A couple may be able to live cheaply in the towns mentioned for a total of around $1400 a month. You should be able to live fairly well for around $1800 a month. That's not bad for a European Mediterranean seaside living lifestyle.

Mountains to Beaches Amazing Cuisine

There are plenty of reasons for considering the beautiful country of Italy, especially for foodies. Each region has its own unique cuisine that uses the primary food sources of the area and has maintained its long-standing tradition, as well as innovations. In Italy you can find authentic delicious Italian dishes and accompany it all with a nice glass of amazing locally produced wine.

In Italy it's also possible to travel from the sea to the mountains, lakes and snow, all in the same region. In a few day's travel, you can go from the cold of the high mountains to a hot beach.

Tradition is still strong in Italy, particularly on the islands like Sardinia and Sicily. It's possible to attend festivals or celebrations identical today to those 100 years ago. It's like traveling back in time.

Art is a strong part of Italy's culture. With its 47 UNESCO sites, 4,700 museums, 200 archaeological sites and the largest collection of works of art in the world, Italy is a paradise for art, culture and history buffs. You can even experience art in some cities without the need to enter a museum, in Rome, Venice, Florence, Palermo, Bologna and Naples, just by taking in the architecture.

Old world craftsmen still exist in Italy. Many dressmakers, shoemakers and other tradesman still make products by hand the same way they've done it for centuries. You can find unique fabrics or find a tailor with 50 years of experience to make you a unique and special dress or suit.

If you have a desire to experience Italy like a

resident, Cagliari in southern Sardinia may be the ideal choice. Temperatures on this island in the Mediterranean are mild all year long. The beach is just 10 minutes from the city's center, and the Mediterranean waters surrounding Italy are said to be especially clean.

The city is very walk-able and bike-able, and it has a great public transport system. There are many public parks. It's not uncommon to see a herd of horses or sheep passing through town.

Want to learn how to cook real Italian food? Sardinian cuisine is said to be truly amazing, from unbelievable appetizers to desserts. Of course, there's always excellent local wines to add to the experience.

The economy in Italy is suffering, just as it is in Spain, but the cost of living in Sardinia is very affordable for a western European country. You should be able to find a comfortable home rental for two people for around $700 a month. You should be able to live a modest but comfortable lifestyle dining out once or twice a week for a total of about $1800 a month—not bad for living in a place with the best Italian food in the world.

Art Culture History and Beaches

Warm weather, beautiful beaches, beautiful islands, ancient history, art and culture: What more could you want? How about world famous Greek hospitality! How could it get any better? How about some of the most delicious and healthiest food in the world? More? Greece has always been something of a bargain. Because of the downturn in Europe and

Greece in particular, the current low cost of living for a country that offers so much makes this a must-visit country.

Some places to consider renting in the Athens area are Agia Paraskeui, Cholargos, and Papagou. They are safe, peaceful areas with many parks. They're also really close to the center of Athens, which is an amazing place to explore.

Renting in these areas can be easy because there are a lot of new properties, and the economic crisis has forced the rental prices to decline. You can rent a pretty nice place for around $400 per month. If your appetite for fun and excitement is high, but your budget is tight, there are communities with denser population and less green space that are even cheaper. Try Cholargos, Agia Paraskevi, Zografou and Ampelokipoi.

It would be hard to find a more exciting place in the world to live for a few months than Athens in Greece, with its excellent food, local wines and some of the best real olive oil in the world. It's the center of art, history and culture. Beautiful beaches and islands. You can experience all this for about $1400 a month, less than what it would cost to live in any rust-belt city in the US. How great is that?

Tropical Island Retirement Dream

Think of exotic tropical islands with everything from volcanoes and bright green rice fields to crowded mega-cities and amazing beaches. You can actually retire to a beach on a tropical island, even if it's just for a few months. The best thing is that the Philippines can be a very budget-friendly place to live.

Many cities in Metro Manila are extremely crowded, but there are still average or mid-sized towns where retired couples can live without worrying about high expenses and natural disasters. The Philippines can be hit regularly by typhoons, just as Florida normally gets unwelcome visits from hurricanes.

Marikina City is an average-sized town where you'll find shopping malls, restaurants, churches, schools, markets, parks and resorts. The best part of this city is Marikina Heights, not just because you can find mixed-culture diners around the town, but also because it is 100% flood free since it is not located in a low-lying area. This town is also peaceful and quiet except for the sound of tricycles, which are used as the main transportation in the vicinity.

Cainta is also a good place to stay, but it's more urban. Although some areas of this town flood easily, many mid- and high-rise condominiums are available very near supermarkets, schools, malls and hospitals.

Tagaytay is the ideal retiree's haven, but prices are higher here, mainly because it's a popular tourist area. Tagaytay has perfect cool climate, clean air, terrific water views, impressive parks and scenic spots.

Other nearby towns like Marikina and Cainta would be good choices with the cost of living just the same as living in the metro area. A couple could live here for about $1200 a month—again, not bad for an exotic tropical island where the English language is widely spoken and understood. One important consideration is that the government is battling rebels on islands remote from the Manila area and the towns mentioned above. A check of travel sites shows there still are many people there who aren't concerned, but check the US State Department and other sites to make your own informed decision.

Inexpensive Exotic Tropical Island

Like the Philippines, it may take a little longer to get to Malaysia because it's on the other side of the world from the US, but Malaysia may be easier to adjust to once you arrive because English is widely spoken there. English is a mandatory subject in school and the main language in Malaysia's colleges and universities. Malaysia is also among the least expensive places to live in the world. Food in Malaysia is cheap, abundant and delicious.

A couple could live in Malaysia for as little as $1200 a month. The cost would be higher in larger cities like Kuala Lumpur, Shah Alam, Penang and Johor Bahru. It is, however, a lot cheaper in the smaller cities like Malacca, Kuantan and Ipoh.

Because Malaysia is an Islamic country, expressing political and sexual liberty is not looked upon favorably. For this reason, many expats chose to live in Penang, which in most cases is more liberal than the rest of the country. The cost of living on the island is pretty high by Malaysian standards, but if that's a problem, one can opt to live on Seberang Prai, a less costly part of the state of Penang.

Someone staying in Penang will likely find plenty of expats and retirees living there to socialize with, including many from the US. Because of the Malaysian government's campaign of "Malaysia My Second

Home," it can be easier to live in Malaysia as a resident than it would be in many other countries.

Penang, Malacca and Sabah are the top choices among expats, Penang for its dizzying variety of food and night life, Malacca for its history, culture and kind people, and Sabah for its fun. Malaysia is inexpensive and exotic, and English is widely spoken, but check the US State Department site for travel advice before heading there because there are parts of the country you will want to avoid. Still, an exotic island that's one of the least expensive places to "live" with beautiful beaches where English is widely spoken is a powerful draw.

Beaches Historic Cheap and Close

Yes, there was a short war fought here decades ago, but since then Nicaragua has become known as the safest country in Central America. Tourism to the country is growing, but the cost of living is the lowest of any country you'll find close to home. The combination of safety, inexpensive living, and closeness to home is appealing.

The weather in Nicaragua is warm in the winter and hot the rest of the year. The lifestyle is laid back and mellow, even compared to the Keys in Florida. A nice apartment in a decent neighborhood can be had for about $400 a month. Groceries for a full month will run about $200, and transportation will cost another $100. A couple could live here for a few months for about $1000-1200 a month.

Yes, Nicaragua is relatively safe, cheap and close to home, but it's not Europe. Many areas are underdeveloped and severely impoverished. Public transportation can be a mess. As an American, you may be disappointed with services that you take for granted in the US, like fresh clean water and electricity. Internet service in the country does not always work, and when it does, it can be very slow.

Nicaragua does have some amazing beaches. Granada is a beautiful, historic colonial town and probably the most popular spot for American expats in the country. The city of Leon would be another city worth considering. San Juan del sur, near the most popular beaches in the country, may be the best choice for water-lovers, but it will cost more too.

Because Nicaragua isn't as developed as the US or most of Europe, it may not be for everyone. For the very adventurous, a few months in this developing country may be a great experience, especially during the winter when the weather is warm. It's hard to beat a safe, inexpensive location close to home, especially when you can live for $1200 a month or less.

RV Retirement Lifestyles

Ultimate Flexibility and Freedom

You only live once, and I'll bet there are places in the United States that you would love to see, but never had the chance to—until now. The job requirement of your next job, retirement, is to enjoy life, so it's time to have fun, stay healthy, and experience some of that freedom this country has been fighting to preserve for us. Becoming a full-time RV'er may just be the perfect lifestyle for you for the first few years of your retirement.

There can be tremendous tax, financial and other advantages once you chose to make a lifestyle of exploring North America full-time. You can choose a new "home" state, one that doesn't have a personal income tax and does have lower auto insurance rates. We'll talk more about that latter.

Have you ever wanted to visit;

1) Yellowstone National Park in Wyoming—High mountain peaks, multicolored bubbling pools, hot springs, pristine lakes and yes, buffalo really still do roam here.

2) The Great Smoky Mountains in Tennessee and North Carolina—Where else can you find 800 miles of trails in a park that's been designated as a World Heritage Site and International Biosphere Reserve?

3) Grand Canyon National Park—Enjoy hiking and backpacking (no, you are not too old), raft the spectacular Colorado River, or just soak up the majestic scenery and feel a sense of true relaxation wash over you as you connect with nature as you never have before.

4) Redwood National and State Park—See the tallest trees on earth up close. Take a hike (there are both long and short trails) and take in the exhilarating relaxing view of the California Pacific Ocean coastline. If you've only seen the Atlantic east coastline, you owe it to yourself to take a trip out west.

There are 58 National Parks in the US. If you include all the battlefields, historic sites, lake-shores, military parks, monuments, recreation areas, scenic rivers, seashores, trails, and the White House, there are 401 sites and 84 million acres to see. When you add in all the state parks, tourist areas, festivals and more that this country has to see and experience, you realize just how much more exciting retirement can be than sitting on the couch watching daytime TV programming.

People Love This Why Not You

Remember how exciting it was to plan a one-week vacation when you were working? Imagine planning the trip of a lifetime where you make a list of all the places you would really love to visit in the US, buy a RV and just go. You could include places with large festivals, museums, race tracks or wherever and whatever you are most interested in.

RV's offer the ability for you to take your bikes, skis, and anything else you need to fulfill the responsibility of your new job and exercise to enjoy great health. Some RV's tow an enclosed trailer so they can bring all of their toys with them everywhere they go.

Be Where The Weather is Always Perfect

Are you tired of shoveling snow? When you become a full-time RV'er, you can winter in Florida, Texas or Arizona, where the weather is warm and sunny. Rental rates for winter RV sites can be found for $500 a month or less, plus electric. These RV parks usually have pools, clubhouses and planned social and recreational events. RV owners are some of the most relaxed and friendly people you'll ever meet. Why not? Enjoying a fantastic lifestyle brings out the best in people.

When those hot weather states start to heat up in the spring, you can head north where the temperatures are more comfortable to watch spring unfold. You can spend summer in the mountains where it's cooler and less humid.

When you're a full-time RV-er, you'll never have to suffer through another miserable hot, humid summer or cold snowy winter unless that's what you want. If you do it right, you may never have to use your heat or AC because the nights will be cool, great for sleeping, and the days pleasantly warm.

Discover Your Perfect Place to Retire

Most people won't live the full-time RV lifestyle for decades. What if there's a town that would be the absolute best place for you to retire, but you've never been it to yet? Well, full-time RV'ing is your opportunity to stay in, see and explore some of the best states and towns to retire mentioned in this book. Full-time RV'ing allows you the opportunity to locate your ultimate place to retire once you're ready to settle down.

Exploring the Possibility

Because of our ancestry, we all have a little nomad blood in us. Maybe this is exactly the best retirement lifestyle for you at this time, but you'll never realize it unless you look into it further. Visiting a few RV dealers, taking test rides and learning more about it is all free, so why not?

Many people who do decide to RV full-time plan whirlwind trips that pack in lots of places to visit while spending only a short time in each place. Full-time RV veterans suggest you consider staying longer in some areas so you can get a good feel for the place. You may not want to stay too long in tourist areas, but you may want to stay for a few months in places that you discover that may make a great place to settle down and retire.

Choosing State Residency

Experts estimate that there are hundreds of thousands of full-time RV'ers, and most of them are retired. There are well established services that provide RV-ers with mail and residency help. Most of these services are based in Florida, Texas and South Dakota, all states without a personal income tax.

Each state has its advantages and disadvantages, and a short visit to the state you choose is required to get things set up. What you'll be doing is the same thing you'd be doing if you moved to any state. You would get driver's licenses, vehicle registration, insurance, register to vote if you wish, and more. The one additional item would be mail service.

This all may sound like a lot of work, but these RV services are there to help you take care of everything. Some new full-timers sell their home and travel to one of these states and buy their RV there. They then take a few days to get mail service and all the legal paperwork taken care of and begin their freedom, having to return to their new "home" state only every few years.

The exact details on how to go about this process are beyond the scope of this book, but you will find links to the best mail and residency services, internet and TV service information for RV-ers, RV videos and more at: www.bestplacestoliveretire.com

Summary and Tips

1) Rather than planning a whirlwind trip with stays of just days or weeks in each place, consider staying at least a month, and three

months may be better. You'll get better rates at the resorts/campgrounds, and you'll spend less money on gas.

2) If you plan on relocating for retirement, consider working possible towns into your travels. You'll get a better idea of what living there is really like. Does the place have the type of shops, restaurants, art, culture, festivals or outdoor recreation that you are looking for?

1) Take the pressure off of making a decision to full-time RV. Most people do it for only 3-4 years, so you're really making a decision of fun, freedom and adventure for only the next few years.

2) Consider buying the smallest RV that you feel will meet your needs. If you do it right, you'll always be where the weather is great and won't be spending much time indoors.

3) If you plan on relocating or "right" sizing, consider selling your home if you own and cash in on the tax-free profit home sale exclusion, before you leave begin RV'ing. You may want to choose a better "home" state.

Live As if You Were Rich

An Excellent Retirement Lifestyle Option

Tired of shoveling snow and cold winters? Think you have to sell your home and move south to solve your problem? Owning in a warmer state in addition to your home state may be your best retirement lifestyle option, and no, you don't have to be a Rockefeller to pull it off.

Many people can't imagine ever living anywhere while renting again after owning their own home for so long. If that's you, this may be a great option. You can forget about shoveling snow during the winter months because you'll be at your "winter home" down south where it's sunny and warm. When it starts to get too hot and muggy there, you can summer in your cooler, less humid northern home.

It's Low Risk

Owning a home where you have family and other ties and a home in a warmer location offers an almost perfect retirement lifestyle. It's also extremely low risk. Why? Because almost all of the reasons people regret moving to a warm location for full-time retirement are eliminated. You'll never have to live where it's too hot or too cold again. Missing family and friends won't be a problem. You'll still have a home near them, so you can be there to share life's special moments like school graduations, Thanksgiving and Christmas.

Many people with two homes spend roughly six months a year at each place. Most people let the weather decide where they'll be living. Getting too hot or muggy in the warm location? Head north. Many people stay there until after the holidays, then join the millions of others heading south to ride out the winter in the sunshine.

It's High Reward

One of the biggest evils facing retirees is boredom. When you own two homes, you will always have a big change of scenery to look forward to that's never farther than a few months away. When most people retiring in place may start dreading the approach of winter, you can look forward to traveling to your winter home, where the fun and festivals are just starting. When the full-time suckers who moved and live full-time in your warmer location start to dread the approach of up to nine months of hot, muggy weather, you'll be looking forward to a beautiful cooler spring weather back home.

It's Healthier

It's a proven fact that outside air is better for your health than breathing indoor air. Places like Florida are perfect during the winter because the humidity is low and it rarely rains. You can spend plenty of time outdoors.

When full-time southern retirees are hiding from heat and humidity inside air-conditioned homes for 7-9 months, you will be in the cooler northern areas and spending far more time outdoors than they are. Sure, there are some hot muggy days in the north too, but anyone who tells you that it's worse in the north doesn't know what they're talking about! The hot weather in "warmer" locations happens every day and night for most of the year.

How to Afford This Lifestyle

I've sold plenty of homes to new retirees who moved to Florida and bought large homes. Many did so because they were going to live in Florida full time, and buying roughly the same size home as they lived in before just made sense to them. Some even bought larger homes because they sold in a high-cost area to move to Florida and had extra cash to buy a larger place. Did this make them happy?

You'd be surprised how many of these people would contact me to sell that big place within just a year or two to downsize. Many reasons were given such as they didn't retire just to spend their time cleaning a big place. Or they realized that they never use more than half the home, but have to shell out cash to cool and pay taxes on the whole house. It was costing more than they counted on, and much of the home was never used.

Still others bought larger than they needed so they would have room when company came down to visit. Those visits were less frequent than they thought, or never happened at all. They couldn't justify paying higher taxes and other costs for 52 weeks a year just to have extra space for a week or two when company was actually there. Thus they lost money to sell the big place they didn't need, move, and buy a better-sized home. That could have been avoided had they bought the right size home in the first place.

What's my point? Many people who own two homes in different locations find that smaller, easier to care for homes or condos work best. Since you'll be avoiding extreme cold and heat all year, you'll be spending more time outdoors. Less time indoors means you probably don't need as big a home as you would if you were indoors hiding from the cold all winter in the north or soaking up the AC avoiding brutal 6-9 month long humid summers in hotter locations.

Actually, you can lower your winter heating bill by heating your northern home just enough to keep the pipes from freezing, while living in the South where you won't need the AC or heat in the winter. With the use of a humidistat, you can keep your cooling cost of your home in the warmer location low. The AC will go on only to keep the humidity from getting too high, not to cool.

Selling Your Current Home and Taking Advantage of the $500,000 Exclusion

If you can afford it and you want to keep your current home and buy a small vacation home or condo in a warmer climate, that's just one of your options. You may want to consider the advantages of selling your current home and cashing in on the $500,000 tax-free home profit exclusion. You could use the proceeds to purchase two right-sized homes. One strategy is to replace your current home with one located in a less expensive town within an hour's drive.

For instance, in the area where most of my family is still located, housing costs are rather high. It's about an hour's drive to both the New York and Philadelphia Metro areas. In less than an hour's drive in the opposite direction from those cities, there's a mountainous resort area popular with outdoor enthusiasts where the home prices are far more reasonable. Located in a more mountainous area, it's also a little cooler in the summer too.

If you like the idea of owing two homes but want to keep your cost low, is there a small, friendly town within a short drive where you could save on housing costs? If it's in a small town with a relaxed pace, it may be better for retirement than where you live now anyway. If it's in the mountains where the summers are a little cooler, all the better. Is it possible that you can own two "right sized" homes for what you could sell the home you now live in for?

43

Buying More Time and Less Chores

Living in a home with a big yard is great when you have kids that use it to play football in. When the kids are gone, though, that big yard just means more of your time spent cutting it. You may want to consider the advantages of living in a downtown area of a nearby small, friendly, safe town. You could walk to shops, restaurants and pubs. You'll save on gas, get exercise, and breathe healthy outdoor air.

You may even want to buy an in-town home with a yard so small it could be landscaped with stone, evergreen plants and pavers to transform it into a great outside space with no grass to cut. Maybe there's an inexpensive lake resort community where the homes don't even have lawns, just trees. In these areas it's all nature except the roads, your driveway and the walkways to your doors.

Your Winter Get-Away Home

The key here is to buy just enough home or condo to be comfortable. Remember, if you do it right you'll be spending less time indoors and more time outdoors because you'll always be where the weather is ideal. Yes, you'll be golfing, biking, going to festivals and generally enjoying life in a comfortable climate when the folks back home are cooped up inside trying to stay warm or cool.

Many of the newer homes have higher ceilings, open floor plans and sliding glass doors that all make a home feel larger than they are. Homes with beautiful areas to spend outdoors in can make a home live larger. Outdoor furniture that's the same as you'd find in a living room or family room is very popular because it allows you to spend more time outdoors more comfortably.

Save on Taxes

Another advantage of owning two homes is using the one in the state with the lowest (or no) personal income tax as your primary residence. Your primary state is where you register your cars and maintain a driver's license. If you own homes in different states, you can choose the one with the best tax benefits, lower car insurance or lower sales tax as your primary residence for tax purposes. Can owning a home in a low or no personal income tax state help you afford two homes?

Summary and Tips

- Consider right-sizing if you own a home larger than you need, especially if you have significant amount of equity in the home and can take advantage of the IRS's gift of tax-free profit of up to $500,000. There's no guarantee how long that gift will be continue to be available to you.
- Consider a home in a less expensive area within an hour of where you now live, if they exist. A less expensive home with less maintenance or a condo (read the condo warning in this book first) can make retirement more comfortable and fun.
- Consider buying a one-story home with few steps even if you're in good health now. Such homes will hold their value better and

appreciate faster as the nation's population ages over the next couple of decades.

- Consider choosing a warmer state that has no or low personal income tax rates and better asset protection for its citizens. Texas and Florida would both be excellent choices for this purpose.
- Consider choosing the closest best state to make travel between two homes less costly and time consuming.

Escaping Winter When You Want

Tired of cold winters and shoveling snow? Then becoming a "snowbird" may be a perfect retirement lifestyle for you. This option is best for people who are happy with where they live overall, but find the winters harder to take every year and or have strong family ties to the area.

Being a snowbird means that for a month to three months every winter, you travel to a warmer destination and live like a local in a fully furnished home or condo rental. These places are usually referred to as seasonal rentals. Almost all winter destinations worthy of escape from the cold have plenty of them available. They come in all different sizes, locations and pricing. It's possible to find fully furnished homes that are more comfortable than hotels, and often for far less cost per month.

Let the Landlord Fix it

The great thing about heading to a warmer climate to live in a fully equipped turnkey home is that you have to pack only your toothbrush and your bathing suit. When you arrive at your warm weather location, you just unpack and enjoy yourself. It's a rental, so if anything breaks or needs attention you just call whoever manages the property to get it fixed. It's their problem, not yours, and they'll fix for you at no charge.

The rental snowbird option offers you an extremely flexible lifestyle. The most popular months for snowbirds are generally January through March. Most seasonal rentals have a minimum rental period of at least one month. These are usually better places to stay than those that rent by the week. Weekly rentals can take a beating, and you are more likely to be next door to rowdy vacationers, than in a place that has a minimal rental period of a least a month. People who can afford to go somewhere for at least a month are usually fellow retirees or independent business people.

The One-Month Wonder

For some people, spending just one month where it's warm and sunny was enough to take the bite out of winter. Many snowbirds are home with family for the holidays, but leave for the beach January 1st for their snowbird location. After going home on February 1st, they have to get through only about another month of winter. For other snowbirds, especially if money isn't an issue, stay two or three months.

That's the beauty of being a snowbird. You can experiment and stay as long or as little as you want, to find what works for you. You could spend one winter at the beach and the next year stay near theme or national parks. You could spend every year at a different warm location doing a different activity and explore the whole US over the course of retirement.

You could even spend a month in a snowy ski town snowmobiling and skiing to add in some variety. You might go overseas for a month, and actually, you could snowbird overseas every year and explore places like Ecuador or Greece.

Seasonal rentals are less costly than staying in a hotel for a month. You can shop at the local supermarkets and make meals at "home" if you wish, as your rental will have all the pots, pans and usually everything you could possibly need, including a grill. Seasonal rentals are usually located in tourist areas of town, but you'll usually be able to find homes available in quieter residential locations too.

Booking well in advance is advised. Booking through a licensed real estate agency with a large choice of seasonal rentals in the area you are interested in is usually the safest way to book. It's easy to do now, thanks to the internet. Many websites have all the information you need, including pictures and sometimes videos of available homes online for you to view.

Low Risk

Have you been thinking of moving somewhere "warm" full-time for retirement? Do you have concerns about moving away from your kids, grand-kids, other family and friends? You're not alone. Becoming a snowbird eliminates those concerns, and you won't have to worry about shoveling snow anymore. How great is that?

Cost

Unless you have money to burn, consider renting the most reasonable place you can, to start with. Renting a small, comfortable, inexpensive place may be your best move because if you do it right, you'll be outside enjoying the great weather most of the time. When you're at the beach or theme park, your experience will be the same at that moment whether you paid $2500 or $25,000 to be in that warm town for the month.

Summary and Tips

- Snowbird areas can get extremely congested during the winter. To avoid the traffic jams and parking hassles, try renting within walking or biking distance of the restaurants, cafes, shops, beach or wherever you'll be spending most of your time.
- Consider renting the smallest, least expensive winter home or condo that will be comfortable because if you do it right, you will not be spending much time indoors.
- While in your snowbird location, on rainy days call a realtor to show you other rentals that may be better choices for next season. There are almost always better locations for less money.

How to Enjoy Warm Winters and Mild Summers

Possibly the Best Retirement Lifestyle You Never Considered

This option is snowbirding, but doesn't involve owning two homes or renting one. With this option, you purchase an RV and use it to travel to and stay in a warm location during the winter. Snowbirding in an RV can offer you more flexibility and could possibly be less expensive.

Investing in an RV can make traveling back and forth much more comfortable. You won't have to worry about getting bed bugs from sleeping in a hotel, and no matter where you are, you can always sleep in your own bed. Getting tired while on a long trip? Just pull into a rest area, truck stop or many Walmart parking lots and take a nap.

No matter where you travel, you'll always have your own bed, bathroom and shower. You'll also always have a kitchen fully equipped the way you like it, complete with refrigerator, stove and microwave. You can equip your entire RV with all the comforts of home.

Stay Anywhere Flexibility

Tired of shoveling snow? No Problem: Go online and book a place to stay in a warmer climate like the beach or near the theme parks for a month or three. Always wanted to see some beautiful national parks in a hot state? Again, not a problem: Make reservations to go during the winter months when the weather is warm.

RVing combines the comfort of home and the benefits of camping. You can go to the beach during the day, and go home to your campsite in the evening and make a gourmet meal that you can enjoy by an outdoor fire under a sky filled with stars.

Just as some people who rent seasonal rentals find one they really like and return year after year, RV-ers often stay at the same RV resort too. The difference is that RV parks often have pools, clubhouses, and planned social activities that make it easy to meet new friends. Most RV owners are very friendly and often walk or bike to the amenities, so you get to know your neighbors because you see them all the time. Many long-term friendships began in RV resorts.

Year Round Use

Experiencing a particularly hot summer at your

northern home? With an RV, you can head north or to the mountains to enjoy cooler, healthier weather. With an RV and a sense of adventure, you can experience an exciting retirement while visiting the most beautiful natural environments this country has to offer, all at an affordable price.

Travel at its Best

When you own a self-contained RV, you'll always be traveling with everything you need. Are you on a special diet? Want to eat healthier while traveling than stopping at those fast food joints along the highway? No problem. Your partner can make something to eat, and you don't even have to stop traveling.

Hate using the sometimes less than sanitary public restrooms at rest areas or restaurants while on the road? Ever worry about who slept in that hotel bed just hours before you? Well, with an RV, you'll always have your own sheets and pillows and everything in your traveling home.

In fact, RV's can offer you more freedom than you've ever experienced before because you can travel anytime you wish. You don't have to have reservations. If you get tired, you can stay in the RV parking area at night at many truck stops for free while traveling. With a built-in automatic generator, you'll always have electric, no matter where you are. Just set the thermostat, and the AC or heat will keep you comfy while parked overnight.

All the Comforts of Home

In just about any place you could possibly want to visit, you'll find campgrounds or RV resorts that offer full hookups of water, sewer, electricity and even internet service. You can stock your fridge and cabinets with all of your favorite foods and cook with utensils and eat and drink from dishes and glasses of your own choosing. While you'll no doubt occasionally want to eat meals at restaurants, you can save money and eat healthier meals when you cook at "home." You can stock the cabinet with your favorite wine, scotch or beer.

Almost everyone I know with RV's outfits their rig with everything they need so they can leave for an adventure on a whim. Summer and Snow birding in an RV may be just the lifestyle perfect for you.

Summary and Tips

- Don't buy at the first RV show or dealer you visit. It takes time to learn what type and size RV might be right for you, and it's a big investment. Look at lots of RV's, take lots of test drives, and talk to lots of people until it becomes clear to you what might be best.

- Consider buying the smallest, least expensive RV that you think will be comfortable for you. It's easier to trade up (many people will) than to trade down, especially if you bought new. Remember, if you're doing things right, you'll be outside enjoying great weather most of the time, not sitting inside.

- Get insurance quotes before you buy. Take the RV's MPG into consideration. Determine the full cost of ownership so you can make the wisest decision. While taking on new debt may not be the smartest thing to do when retiring, the interest on a RV loan may be tax deductible if it qualifies as a second home, and most do. Consult a tax pro for specifics.

Moving for Retirement

Risk: High for Buyers Low for Renters

Moving a long distance for permanent full-time living can pose the biggest risk to enjoying your retirement if the place you move to turns out to be a place you come to hate. This happens more often than new retirees realize. Let's take a quick look at Florida, a state that for decades was the default destination for retirees if they weren't going to retire in place.

A University of Florida study published in 2009 documented nearly 13 million people moving to Florida from other US states, and nearly 10 million moving out of Florida to other states, during the study period. That churn of people moving in and out of Florida is great for real estate brokers, but it was devastating emotionally and financially to many of the people who did all that buying, selling and long-distance moving. I know: I hold a Florida real estate broker's license and saw a lot of misery first hand.

Reducing Retirement Relocation Risk

By the time you finish this book, you'll learn how to lower the risk of any move to another US state, thereby increasing your odds of long-term success. One way is to consider selling all of your furniture and buying new in your new location, especially if you're moving to the mountains or beach. The furniture you now own now might not look right in that new log cabin in the mountains or condo near the beach.

Selling your current furnishings (except prized possessions, of course) will greatly reduce the hassle and expense of long-distance moving. It will eliminate the stress from housing availability delays and having a rented truck full of furniture and nowhere to go with it. Buying new furniture in the area you're moving may help you enjoy your new more because the furnishings will match the area better. How much is that old dirty washer and energy wasting dryer worth anyway? How much will it cost you to move it 1000 miles? It might be better to buy brand new, more energy efficient

If you're going to sell your furniture, why not consider renting a seasonal rental in the area you're moving to give yourself more time to find the right home with less stress and pressure. You are likely to need time to learn the nicer areas, real estate prices, what type of home is best, etc.

States With the Highest Quality of Life

How States Were Rated

I gathered data, statistics and ratings mostly from government sources, but also from trusted nonprofit and other organizations that concern themselves with factors that influence our quality of life. Just some of the factors I considered were cost of living, health care access, health care quality, health wellness, property crime rate, tax burden, violent crime rate and well-being data.

I believe the following list shows the true best places to retire because it uses more quality of life factors than most. There may be places that are far more popular for vacations, but just having a hundred million visitors a year doesn't automatically make a state a great place to live. In fact, sharing the roads, restaurants and special outdoor areas with hoards of tourists who are just in your neighborhood to party while on vacation, then leave, may affect your quality of life in a negative way.

Although I used sunshine as a factor in ranking US states, I did not use temperature. This is a factor that almost every other so-called "best places to" list uses, especially for retirees, but I think it leads to faulty results. For example, I recently saw one "best places to retire" list that described how they used the weather factor as "the warmer the better." In that case, Death Valley, California would be the place that wins the weather category on that list because the temperature there reaches 120 degrees or more for 5-20 days every year.

I don't use temperature as a factor because the ideal place temperature-wise for humans is between 68-72 degrees with low humidity, all year round. There just isn't a place like that in the US with the possible exception of a very expensive sliver of real estate along the southern California coast. Other than that, when people move to where it's warm during the winter, they pay for those three months of glorious weather with up to nine months of unbearable heat the rest of the year, along with bugs, snakes and other pests all year long. That's why millions of people have permanently retired to warm winter states, only to move back. Selling, moving long distance, buying where it's "warm," then selling and moving long distance back to where you started costs about $100,000-$250,000.

Am I trying to talk you out of moving to a warm

winter state? Absolutely, if you will end up being one of the people who lose time (time is life, and we get only so much, so if you waste time, you waste life) and a fortune to move somewhere, only to learn they hate it. If your life will improve by moving to a warm winter state, then I absolutely want you to do that. But how do you know what's going to happen before you move? I thought you'd never ask. You are going to learn what your odds of loving or hating a place likely are *before* you move there. Let's get started.

How to Use The Best States to Retire List

The best way to explain how to use this book's best states list to take the risk out of moving for retirement, is to do two actual comparisons. The first comparison is for Herman and Lilly Bumplestien (the names are made up, but the comparisons are real). The Bumplestiens currently live in Connecticut, but are thinking of selling their home next spring after they retire and move to Florida.

Mr. Bumplestien is tired of shoveling snow. He has the money to buy a snow-blower, but as we all know, it's physically painful for people from New England to spend money. Lilly always loved the beach on vacations and would like to live close enough to one in Florida that she could go every day if she wanted. Let's use this book to compare the state of Connecticut to Florida to see what the chances are of the Bumplestiens being happy with a move to the sunshine state.

Overall List Rank: Florida #31 / Connecticut #47

Score one for a move to Florida. After all of the quality of life factors were analyzed, Florida ranked higher than Connecticut. While a ranking of #31 for Florida is nowhere near the top states in quality of life factors, it is an improvement from Connecticut, and that's likely all they'll notice. Herman and Lilly will likely be happy with a better overall quality of life. Why does Florida rank better than Connecticut on my list in this book?

- Because according to available data, that you can check for yourself by following the resource links in this book, Florida has a lower cost of living than Connecticut.
- Florida has a better well-being score.
- Florida's tax burden is much lower.
- Florida has more days of sunshine.

Asset Protection: Florida AAA / Connecticut ACF

Score another one for a move to Florida for the B'steins because Florida's state laws will protect their assets better than if they stayed in Connecticut. This is good news for Herman and Lilly because their home has appreciated nicely over the years, and they own it free and clear. The asset protection score will be explained shortly.

Gun Laws: FL-Strong Gun Rights / CT-Strong Gun Control

Mr. & Mrs. B never considered learning about the

firearm laws in Florida. This could be a problem for them because they both strongly believe that gun control makes people safer. Over one million people in Florida have a permit to carry a concealed weapon, and tourists can conceal weapons when visiting Florida if they have a permit in their home state. Florida has legalized the use of silencers for hunting and says that gun owners have the right to set up a gun range in their backyard. The Bumplestiens should have decided to look into Florida's gun laws further.

Marijuana

Florida: Medical—No/Decriminalized—No

Connecticut: Medical—Yes/Decriminalized—Yes

The Bumplestiens are old hippies and would love to smoke a little marijuana if it were legal to do so, but that doesn't matter since it's not totally legal in either state; however, Mrs. B does suffer from a chronic disease, and her Connecticut doctor has already talked about prescribing marijuana rather than toxic opiates if her pain continues to get worse. This won't be an option if they move to Florida.

Gallup Poll: Florida 46% / Connecticut 31%

The B'stiens went to the resource website and learned that 46% of Floridians think their state is the best or at least one of the best to live in. While this is nowhere near the resident satisfaction rate of best-ranked states, it's better than Connecticut's 31%: another vote for going to Florida.

Mr. & Mrs. B are leaning toward a move to Florida because most of the lights are green, and they believe they can deal with the gun and medical marijuana issues. They have also decided to buy and read the "Florida Move Guide" to make sure they consider everything before actually signing a listing agreement to put the house up for sale. That's good, because they'll learn that Herman's dream of playing lots of golf and Lilly's desire for living at the beach may not turn out as they're picturing it.

A Completely Different Comparison

Maureen Whipple (the names and characters are made up, but the state comparisons are real) is from New Hampshire and has been a widow now for a couple of years. She and her husband retired at 62, but unfortunately Mr. Whipple passed away unexpectedly just a few months afterwards. Maureen has been thinking about moving to Florida for a fresh start because although she has children and grand-kids in the area, she doesn't get out of the house much. She also now dreads the approach of winter. Let's see how Hew Hampshire stacks up against Florida.

Overall List Rank: New Hampshire #6-65% /Florida #31-40%

Ms. Whipple did not believe that New Hampshire had a higher quality of life than Florida, so she followed the links in the resource section of this book, and this is some of what she found:

- According to the US Department of Health and Human Services, New Hampshire's health care quality score is over 50% better than Florida's score.

- Her overall tax burden is lower than it would be if she moves to Florida.
- New Hampshire bests Florida in the basket of health and happiness measurements that make up a Well-being score.
- The property crime rate in Florida is considerably higher than it is in New Hampshire, and the violent crime rate in Florida is more than double the rate it is where she lives now.

Another big surprise came when she learned that 46%, or less than half of Floridians, felt that Florida was the best or one of the best states to live in. But over two thirds, 67% of New Hampshire residents, think their state is the best or at least one of the best. With winter approaching and a move to Florida not looking as appealing as it did before she started to research the move, she was feeling a little depressed, and then ....

How to Look Forward to Winter

Maureen got to the part of this book that recommends people try out new things to help them develop their retirement plan (which has nothing to do with financial retirement planning). While talking to her son, she mentioned that this book suggested trying a "learn to ski" day, telling her son she could never do that. Her granddaughter overheard, and although she was a snowboarder, not a skier, suggested that they try the "learn to ski" pass together.

They went, and Maureen loved it.

Maureen went again just a couple of days later because the ski area was just a half hour away, and she wanted to see if she actually loved skiing, or if it was really just spending the day with her granddaughter that she enjoyed so much the first day. Maureen enjoyed it even more because she was less fearful, was able to turn better, and met and talked with lots of great new people as she rode the slow ski lift to the top of the bunny (beginner) slopes.

She loved it so much that she went to a ski shop and bought her own ski equipment and ski clothes that keep her toasty no matter the temperature. The ski shop owner encouraged her to join the ski club. She did and again met lots of great new friends. That led to her buying a bike and joining the bike club that most of her new ski club friends belonged to.

Now every day, she either skis in the winter or bikes the rest of the year with her new friends and also socializes with them. She now has an active, adventurous, exciting retirement, has lost 30 pounds, and looks great. Now she is one of the millions of people around the world who look forward to winter and snow instead of dreading it. Your results may not be like Maureen's, my made-up example: They may be better.

What if She had Never Tried This?

Although Maureen lives in a state rated better in more quality of life factors and has much better resident ratings, this does not guarantee that moving to that lower-rated state would have been a mistake.

Only you can decide what's best for you. All this book does is help you find the information that's already out there in the hope that can it can help you increase your odds of better enjoying your retirement years.

What if Maureen had never tried skiing or found that it really wasn't for her? Her best bet probably would have been to continue living where her family is and enjoy the months in New Hampshire when the weather is nice. Maybe after spending the holidays with family, she could head to Florida for January through March and become an annual snowbird.

Limitations and a Warning

One thing I learned from selling homes to hundreds of people making permanent moves to paradise, only to turn around and sell to move out, is that many realized after moving 1000 miles away that family mattered more than they realized. Perhaps too they found that frequent travel to remain close was more difficult and disruptive than they imagined before moving. While there were usually multiple reasons why people moved back, missing their long-time friends and family was one of the most prominent reasons.

Tip—If you think missing home might be a problem before you even move, it probably will be. A high percentage of people who mentioned this reason for moving back said they were concerned about it before they moved, but moved anyway to please their spouse or because they weren't sure if it really would be a problem. It was, so much so that they could not enjoy "paradise."

Chance of Long Term Relocation Success

While almost everyone is pleased with their relocation at first, it's the actual quality of life they experience in their new area compared to their last one that will determine how happy they are with their new home as the years pass. Based upon a state's quality of life factors, each state is ranked from one to fifty. The state that had the highest overall score in a large basket of quality of life factors according to the data was ranked as the #1 state to retire in. The state with the lowest score ranked 50th. Each state also has a number that predicts the chances of happiness for people relocating to that state. For example, a state rated at 45% means it's estimated that 45% of people moving to that state for retirement will be happy with their decision long term, and 55% won't.

Improving Your Chances of Success

Regardless of how a particular state rates overall, you can improve your chances of long-term success by relocating to a highly desirable town in that state. Choosing a desirable college, outdoor, or other town that has better quality of life factors and is better liked by residents than the state overall, will improve your odds.

For instance, one reason Florida doesn't rank very high in overall quality of life when compared to others states is the state's crime rate. It's higher than the national average, and therefore worse than most other states. However, if you've decided to move to Florida and choose a town with a much lower crime rate than Florida's average, your decision would increase your chances of success because the overall quality of life score would improve. When researching crime rates, it's best to look at and compare the actual data for yourself. There's a link to a tool that will allow you find the crime rate for any town in the US, and even a map of the higher and lower crimes areas in the towns, at:

www.bestplacestoliveretire.com

Asset Protection Score

Every state determines how well or poorly its citizens' assets, such as the equity in their home or IRA balance, are protected by that state's laws. You've probably scrimped and saved all your life so you can enjoy a retirement free from the stress of money problems; however, in some states a lawsuit resulting from an accident or other financial calamity could ruin your 50 years of retirement planning by allowing a creditor to take your home, retirement funds and income. In other states a creditor won't be able to touch your IRA's, home or certain other assets.

This asset protection is not the result of fancy expensive legal maneuvers that a citizen must take. It's just automatic protection of your money when you're a resident of some states. This information could help you if you're torn between moving to two similar states, but asset protection in one state is fantastic and the other one offers little or no real protection. The information we provide is not legal advice, and laws can change, so keep that in mind in case you want to consult with a licensed attorney in the state(s) you're considering relocating to.

Asset protection scores are provided for information

purposes only and did not affect how a state was ranked.

Marijuana

A recent study showed that states with laws that allow doctors to prescribe medical marijuana for pain instead of addictive opiates such as Oxycontin have lower accidental deaths and other problems associated with addiction to dangerous prescription drugs. Other studies have shown that 4 out of 5 heroin addicts in the US started using it only after becoming hooked on doctor-prescribed drugs. After the patients were no longer able to get a refill prescription, they turned to the illegal market and started using heroin to satisfy their addiction instead.

As we age, we're more likely to develop chronic medical conditions where pain can be managed only by the strongest pain medications. Currently, many of the most powerful prescription drugs are made from the same plant that heroin is and are just as addictive. Some states have approved medical marijuana so doctors have the choice to prescribe that instead.

The state list includes a simple yes or no on whether a state has approved medical marijuana as a treatment option by licensed physicians. State medical marijuana "yes or no" is provided as additional information only, and *did not* affect how a state was ranked.

Recreational Marijuana

If you're an old hippie, maybe you'd like the freedom to smoke a little pot occasionally, if it were legal. Or maybe you're one of the millions of regular smokers in the US who enjoys pot despite it being illegal to do so in most states. You may want to know how the state you're thinking of moving to treats non-violent pot smokers. The information provided relates to the possession of small amounts of marijuana for personal use only, and whether its use is illegal, decriminalized or legal in a state.

Recreational marijuana information is provide as additional information only and *did not* affect how a state was ranked.

What do the Residents Think of Their State?

You could make the case that what residents think of their state may be the only factor you really need to know to make a wise decision about moving there or not. For instance, if 75% of residents say their state is a great place to live, the odds are that's how you'll feel too, once you move there and become one of them.

Would you change your entire life and burn a lot of time, effort and money to move to a state where most of the people living there don't like it? Your answer may be "of course not." Yet that's exactly what 1000's of people do every day. Why? Because they didn't even know that this type of information is available.

Take Florida, for example. Somewhere close to 500,000 people move there every year, convinced that Florida is the best state to live in. Why else would they spend a fortune to move 1000 miles? Still, a Gallop poll found that 54% of Floridians don't think Florida is the best state to live in *or even one of the best*. That's why millions of people have moved to Florida over the years, only to discover they didn't like it and moved out.

Always Check This

I recommend checking the latest Gallup poll on resident satisfaction. It can give you another indication of whether a move is probably a good idea or may need to be researched further. Find it at:

http://www.bestplacestoliveretire.com/2015/02/best-places-retire-live-quality-life-resources.html

The Best Towns

For most states, I have also included a few towns that I feel would even further improve your chances of a successful relocation to that state. Preferences in the selection of towns include college towns, outdoor towns and towns that score higher overall for that state.

College Towns

Designated by (C), these are towns where college students make up a high percentage of the population of the city or town. College towns usually are more walkable, safer, and have better public transportation than most towns. They also have lots of restaurants, pubs and shops the students and their families that visit them can enjoy. They are usually more economically stable. To make the list, the town must be safe, so not all college towns make the cut. State College in Pennsylvania, a small town almost out in the middle of nowhere and dominated by Penn State University, would be an example.

Outdoor Towns

Designated by (O), these are towns located in areas known as hubs for outdoor recreation. It could be a beach town with lots of scuba and surf shops. It could be a ski town at the base of a world-class mountain. Outdoor towns have a high percentage of active people who enjoy participating in outdoor sports and staying healthy. They usually have more than their fair share of restaurants, pubs and shops, usually located in a safe, walkable historic downtown. A good example of an outdoor town would be Islamorada, Florida. They must have a low crime rate to make the list in this book.

Overall Great Towns

Designated by (OV), these are towns that had among the highest overall quality of life scores in a state. They are just among the best places to live in that state.

Grand Slam Towns

***If you see this, it means the town is a college town, outdoor town and a great all-around town all rolled into one. Towns like this are extremely rare, but are such amazing places to live or retire that they're worthy of the highest consideration, even if they're located in a lower-ranked state.

Top 10 States for High Retirement Quality of Life

Best State to Live in #10

55% Chance of Successful Long-Term Relocation to Nebraska

Asset Protection Grade: IRAs-F Other-D
Gun Laws: Favors Gun Rights
Medical Marijuana: No
Recreational Marijuana: Decriminalized (first offense only)

A majority of Nebraskans think their state is one of the best places to live in the US. According to a poll done by Gallup, that's better than what most US residents said about their state. Nebraska scores particularly well in quality of health care and well-being and has a very low violent crime rate. The cost of living in Nebraska is among the lowest in the US. Being in the middle of the country creates the perfect stop-over for long road trips for out-of-town friends and a launching point for epic road trips of your own. As one resident of the state told me, "Live in Nebraska and save the coasts for vacation."

If you want to retire where you can enjoy a high quality of life in a safe environment without spending a lot of money, Nebraska is worthy of your consideration.

Nebraska Cities to Consider: Kearney

Kearney (pronounced car-nee), a college town of just 31,000, is home to the University of Nebraska at Kearney.. During the winter months, residents enjoy cross country skiing, sledding and ice skating. Summers bring picnicking, fishing and swimming, hiking and biking, with 17+ miles of concrete paths set aside for hiking, biking and jogging. If you enjoy being out of doors, Kearney has something to please everyone.

Kearny is safe and walkable and has plenty of shops and restaurants to walk or bike to. The median (half the homes sell for less, and half sell for more) home price is about $140,000. Safe, affordable college towns are rare and make great places to retire.

More Top Nebraska Towns

Bellevue (OV) 52,000/$137,000
Columbus (OV) 23,000/$110,000
Fremont (OV) 27,000/$115,000

Papillion (OV) 20,000/$170,000
Valentine (O) 3,000/ $98,000

Best State to Live in #9

60% Chance of Successful Long-Term Relocation to Vermont

Asset Protection Grade: IRAs-B Other-B
Gun Laws: Strongly Favors Gun Rights
Medical Marijuana: Yes
Recreational Marijuana: Decriminalized

Vermont: The Green Mountain State

Vermont is the 6th smallest state in the nation and the 2nd least populated state. The capital of Vermont is Montpelier, the only state capital without a McDonald's and the first state to require GMO labeling. Burlington is its largest city.

Vermont is home to many major ski areas including Killington, one of the largest in the eastern US. Skiing, cross country skiing, fishing, hiking, mountain biking and snowmobiling are just some of the outdoor recreation that's big in a state that's made up of rivers, lakes and mountains. The Green Mountain Range provides scenic views throughout Vermont. Most of the state is made up of forests, and the fall foliage is breathtaking.

Vermont is host to many festivals, including the Vermont Maple Festival, Festival on the Green, and the Apple Festival. The culture and rich history of Vermont also make it an attractive place to visit as well as live. Vermont scores higher than about 80% of the other states in quality of life factors.

Its location in New England makes it a great choice for retirees from the northeast, especially if winter sports will play a big part in keeping you healthy and happy. Taxes in Vermont are fairly high and real estate isn't cheap, but resident satisfaction is among the best in the country. If you can afford it, Vermont is one of the safest, most beautiful places to retire in the northeastern US.

Burlington, VT *** A Grand Slam Town!

Burlington is a picturesque lakeside college town and outdoor town with an award-winning historic downtown. It's home to just over 42,000 people, but it's still the most populated town in Vermont. The University of Vermont, Champlain College and Saint Michael's College make their homes here. The town enjoys a strong sense of community.

The economy is thriving in Burlington. Ben & Jerry's started their business in Burlington in 1978. Other successful businesses are Vermont Teddy Bear Company, Burton Snowboards, and Lake Champlain Chocolates, all headquartered in Burlington.

In the heart of the city is the bustling Historic Church Street Marketplace. It is a pedestrian mall and also the site of many annual festivals. A very popular year-round farmers market is also held here.

The city ranks very high on U.S. lists for having 92% of their residents in good or great health. Obesity rates are low, and so are cases of diabetes. Fletcher Allen Healthcare not only employs the majority of the workforce, but also provides excellent quality healthcare for the area. Burlington's air quality is also

79

among the best in the US.

In Burlington you can walk or bike along the banks of Lake Champlain for miles, kayak, or take a boat cruise on the lake. The local music and art scene thrives in Burlington, and there's no shortage of nightlife, as you might expect in a college town. The food, the breweries, and the pubs are also noted as being world-class in this very safe town. In fact, almost every town in Vermont enjoys low crime rates.

World class ski resorts, cross country trail walking, hiking, biking and other recreational opportunities can help keep you healthy and connected all year round. Burlington is one of the best choices you can make to retire, especially if winter sports will be part of your retirement plan, or you intend to snowbird. It's not cheap to live in a town this great. The median home price is in Burlington is a little over $250.000.

Montpelier, VT (O)

Welcome to one of the smallest, quaintest state capital in the US, and a four-season outdoor town. Only about 8000 people call Montpelier home, and maybe that's why they don't have a McDonald's. This is the state capital that passed the first law requiring the labeling of products made with genetically modified organisms.

If you plan on using winter sports as part of your plan to live a healthier longer life, the nearby major ski areas like Mad River Glen and Sugarbush as well as the cross country trails will make that easy. Actually, you're never far from skiing in any town in this beautiful state.

Summertime brings hiking and biking in the mountains and kayaking in the rivers of the valleys. Outdoor Magazine has named Montpelier as one of the 16 best places to live in the US. I agree. Vermont is clean, beautiful and fun, but it's not inexpensive. Montpelier's median home sale price in north of $250,000.

More Top Vermont Towns

Essex Junction (OV) 10,000/$250,000
Middlebury (C) 7,000/$270,000
St. Johnsbury (OV) 7,000/$155,000

Best State to Live in #8

Recommended Warm/Hot Weather State

65% Chance of Successful Long-Term Relocation to Texas

Asset Protection Grade: IRAs-A Other-A
Gun Laws: Strongly Favors Gun Rights
Medical Marijuana: No
Recreational Marijuana: Illegal

Ah, the great state of Texas—the Lone Star State. Texas is a large state (2nd only to Alaska), and the population of 26 million is spread out over 268,000 square miles. The capital city of Austin is a live music mecca and the 11th most populated city in the states. Texas was formerly an independent republic, gaining its independence from Mexico. Texas is named for the word *Tejas*, which means "friends" in the Caddo language.

Perhaps Texas' greatest strength is its diversity, not only in people, but landscape. In Texas you can see deserts, mountains, prairies, forests, and even a coastline. There is the beautiful hill country and also the rolling plains to admire. You also can't beat the bluebonnets that bloom in the spring.

If you need a job, you can find one. Texas has a very strong economy. Taxes are low in Texas, and it does not have a state income tax.

There are a couple of complaints that come from veteran Texans: the weather and the insects.

Depending on where you live, the weather is very temperamental. It changes in the blink of an eye, and damaging tornadoes and other harsh weather is fairly common. With the weather comes the mosquitoes and the humidity. Flies, wasps, and ants can also be a nuisance to deal with, depending on the season.

In Texas, there is pride. If you jump in and join Texans, you will be welcomed with open arms. They are known for being very friendly and helpful people. The state is very family-friendly, but can also cater to the retired.

Canyon, Texas*** A Grand Slam Town!

Wow. A college town and outdoor town with a median home sale price of just $130,000 is hard enough to find in this country. Add one of the lowest crime rates in the country, and this town of just 14,000, home to West Texas A&M University, adds up to one of the best places to retire in the US if warm (hot?) weather is one of your priorities.

The town gets its name from nearby Palo Duro Canyon State Park. The park features the second largest canyon in the US as well as camping, hiking, horseback riding, picnicking. It's also been named the best place to mountain bike in Texas.

The historic downtown is filled with unique shops, restaurants and watering holes you can walk to after parking the car. Many annual events are held in the town square, such as the Fourth of July celebration, Main Street Concert Series, and a Chamber-sponsored cook off.

Texas offers among the best quality of life and

resident satisfaction ratings in the US. An outdoor college town in the state with home prices far lower than the national average and a very low crime rate all add up to one of the best places to retire in the US. Towns like this are extremely rare and certainly deserve consideration.

More Top Texas Towns

Atascocita (OV) 65,000/$155,000
College Station (C) 95,000/$179,000
Denton (C) 115,000/$150,000
Grand Prairie (OV) 175,000/$125,000
La Porte (OV) 35,000/$120,000
Leauge City (OV) 85,000/$180,000
Midland (OV) 115,$150,000
Mission (OV) 77,000/$95,000
San Marcos (C) 50,000/$125,000
Weatherford (OV) 26,000/$135,000

Best State to Live in #7

65% Chance of Successful Long Term Relocation to Minnesota

Asset Protection: IRAs-F Homestead-A Other-A
Gun Laws: Middle of the Road
Medical Marijuana: Yes
Recreational Marijuana: Decriminalized

Move There for Retirement?

Isn't it too cold up there? The fact is, Minnesota has been named in numerous lists over the last few years as one the best states to live in. It does get cold in Minnesota (though the winters have been getting milder), but the high quality of life makes this state a top place to retire.

Known as the "Land of 10,000 Lakes," Minnesota is one of the most beautiful states in the US. All that water provides lots of outdoor recreation like swimming, fishing and water skiing in the summer and ice skating and ice fishing in the winter. (Admit it, you always wanted to try ice fishing.) This is a top state for cross country skiing and snowmobiling.

One thing that struck me while researching Minnesota is the high number of safe, livable towns. There are probably more small towns that score well because of low crime coupled with lots of amenities than just about any other state.

If you live in Minnesota and are thinking of moving somewhere warmer, chances are your only choices will probably be places that score lower on most quality of life factors than Minnesota does (except "perceived" better weather). Snowbirding during winter while continuing to reside with family and friends in Minnesota should be seriously considered.

Winona, Minnesota

Small towns with colleges make great places to live for retirees. This great little town of just 30,000 is home to Winona State University and St. Mary's University of Minnesota. Like many of Minnesota's towns, Winona has a very low crime rate. It's also a very walkable town with lots of shops and restaurants.

Winona is often referred to as a historic Island town. It's not a true island, but it is surrounded by a river and lakes that offer beautiful water views. As you can imagine, outdoor recreation involving water like kayaking, canoeing, fishing and ice-skating in the winter is big.

Some of the best places to retire are small cities that offer retirees lots of variety and activities. Winona has annual music, film and other festivals for residents to look forward to. There are nearby wineries to tour, boating and marinas. The cross country skiing and snowshoeing are superb during the winter.

Minnesota scores well in all of the quality of life factors that are important to you. Resident satisfaction in the state is high compared to other states. One big advantage Minnesota has over many other states is affordable housing. This great, fun little college town has a median home price of around $145,000. That makes it one of the most affordable places to live year round for retirees. For those who do not like winter sports, Winona would be a great place to live most of the year while snowbirding during the winter.

More Top Minnesota Towns

Ely (O) 4,000/$90,000
Grand Marais (O) 15,000/$210,000
Moorhead (C) 38,000/$150,000
New Ulm (OV) 14,000/$125,000
Northfield (C) 20,000/$210,000
Rochester (OV) 110,000/$165,000
St Cloud (C) 65,000/$155,000
Willmar (OV) 20,000/$134,000

Best State to Live in #6

65% Chance of Successful Long-Term Relocation to New Hampshire

Asset Protection: IRAs-B Other than IRAs-F
Homestead-B
Gun Laws: Favors Gun Owners
Medical Marijuana: Yes
Recreational Marijuana: Illegal

Live Free

The state of New Hampshire is well-known for hosting the New Hampshire primary, the first primary in the U.S. presidential election cycle. It's also worthy of hosting an action-packed four-season retirement lifestyle. The White Mountain Range, rivers, lakes, forests, provide residents of New Hampshire excellent outdoor recreational opportunities, including some of the best skiing in the US. New Hampshire also has a short coastline on the Atlantic Ocean that's a popular summer seaside destination. That's right, major ski resorts for winter fun and seaside towns to visit during the summer in one state.

New Hampshire does not have a state sales tax. It does not have a personal state income tax except on interest and dividends. New Hampshire also has one of the lowest crime rates in US. See a video about New Hampshire at: www.bestplacestoliveretire.com

Berlin, New Hampshire

Choosing to include the town of Berlin in this book

is a departure from the way I picked other towns to feature. If you live or have visited Berlin in the last decade, you may be saying it would be crazy to choose such a "depressed" town as a best place to retire. Berlin was a great little town in the past that grew up around a paper mill that supplied material to newspapers around the country for decades. When that factory closed and sections of it were torn down, it left the city looking as though war had destroyed part of it. So did I lose my mind or drink too much, leading to choosing this scarred town?

The State of New Hampshire offers a very high quality of life, topping just about every other state. It doesn't have a sales tax and doesn't have a personal income tax. Resident satisfaction is higher than just about every other state. The one factor that keeps it from scoring even higher is the cost of housing. The New Hampshire median sale price is $250,000, while the national average is only $185,000. Every town I looked at featuring New Hampshire had homes that were far higher in price than most retirees could afford.

Enter Berlin, New Hampshire, with a median home sale price of only $95,000. Unlike many economically depressed towns across this country, Berlin's crime rate is far lower than the national average. What Berlin offers retirees is a very safe place to live with low home prices in one of the best states with the highest quality of life in the US.

Retirees without deep pockets who move to Berlin will likely enjoy a better quality of life in retirement than they could afford just about anywhere else in the

US, especially if enjoying winter sports or snowbirding will be part of their retirement plan. If enough retirees (who won't compete for full time jobs) move to Berlin and spend their fixed income in this town of just 10,000 people, the town could thrive. Home prices could increase, rewarding the early adapters.

Maybe a developer will turn the vacant land left from the paper mills into something wonderful. The rotting large scar left over from the closing of Bethlehem Steel Corporation was transformed into a Sands Casino, shops, a museum, condos and more in Pennsylvania, a state with far lower quality of life scores than New Hampshire.

Jericho Mountain State Park, the largest ATV park in the northeastern US, just opened a few years back. There are major ski resorts not far from Berlin. If you are looking for a small town with lots of community spirit, a very low crime rate and low home prices in a state with very high quality of life and resident satisfaction ratings, consider Berlin. See a video: http://www.bestplacestoliveretire.com/2014/08/best-state-live-new-hampshire.html

More Top New Hampshire Towns

Dover (OV) 30,000/$240,000
Hanover (C) 9000/$470,000
Plymouth (O) 22,000/$320,000

Best State to Live in #5

65% Chance of Successful Long-Term Relocation to South Dakota

Asset Protection: IRAs-B Non IRA-F Homestead-A
Gun Laws: Strongly Favors Gun Owners
Medical Marijuana: No
Recreational Marijuana: Illegal

South Dakota is one of the largest states by size, but it's one of the least populated, with less than 900,000 people in the entire state. People in South Dakota are friendly, and every town in the state has a small town feel.

Contrary to popular belief, it's not always snowing in South Dakota. In fact, it gets pretty nice during spring and summer. Sure, there's a lot of snow in the winter, but that's a good excuse to bust out the cross country skis and snowmobile.

Sportsmen (and women) find abundant wildlife to hunt from white-tail and mule deer to turkey, pheasants, Canadian geese and ducks. Fishermen have been known to pull nice big walleye out of the glacial lakes and Missouri River reservoirs, and in the Black Hills, Chinook salmon and trout can be had. It's an incredible paradise of outdoor activities all year round.

One of the most popular sports in South Dakota is cycling, and the state is home to the George S. Mickelson Trail, which runs 109 miles through the Black Hills. It's an excellent place to ride your mountain bike, run or just take a walk. Got a competitive streak? Try the annual Mount Rushmore marathon, but be prepared—the elevation is over 4,000 feet and you might feel a little bit of altitude sickness if you're a flat-lander not used to such high ground.

Ever hear about the annual Sturgis Motorcycle Rally? Every year during the first week of August, bikers head out for the biggest motorcycle rally in the world. It's a major event that draws hundreds of thousands of participants from all over the country and the world. The participants outweigh the residents of this tiny little town of just over 6,000 by an overwhelming majority.

The Black Hills of South Dakota are the tallest mountain range east of the Rockies. Thousands of visitors flock to see Mt. Rushmore and the Crazy Horse memorial each year. South Dakota is incredibly beautiful and offers a life of adventure to those who seek it.

South Dakota can make financial sense for retirees because the cost of living is lower than most other places. There is also no personal state income tax. South Dakota's crime rate is very low compared to most other states. This state offers a high quality of life for retirees at a very affordable cost.

Spearfish, SD ***A Grand Slam Town!

For a small town of just 11,000 residents, Spearfish is one of the best outdoor recreation towns in the US. Mountain biking, rock climbing, hiking, and fly-fishing are just some of the activities available for the outdoor lover. Nearby Spearfish Canyon is a scenic and lively place for outdoor enthusiast activities. The great scenery is also excellent for anyone into photography too.

The gorgeous fall foliage around Spearfish attracts visitors and wows the locals. Combined with the waterfalls, limestone cliffs, spruce trees, and pine forests, you will be hard pressed to find a more majestic area.

Spearfish is close to Mount Rushmore, located at the base of the Black Hills. The four year Black Hills State University attracts students who want to attend a small friendly college. The university trains teachers, offers Master's programs, and hosts a summer arts institute.

There are many dining options, charming boutiques and shops, and even a nightlife in Spearfish. There are quality schools and many parks. When you're walking down the street, you will see people you know doing the same. The small-town feel is a big draw to many and you can bike or walk pretty much everywhere.

Spearfish may be small, but it has a lot going on. People who call this place home have no regrets about living in this charming but bustling little town. The median home price in Spearfish is about $170,000, which is high for South Dakota, but not for a Grand Slam Town! See a video about Spearfish go to: http://www.bestplacestoliveretire.com/2014/08/best-small-town-retire-live-spearfish-south-dakota.html

More Top South Dakota Towns

Aberdeen (OV) 26,000/$134,000

Brookings (C) 23,000/$145,000
Sturgis (OV) 7000/#123,000
Vermillion (C) 11,000/$129,000

Best State to Live in the US #4

70% Chance of Successful Long-Term Relocation to Colorado

Asset Protection: IRAs-A Non-IRA-F Homestead-D
Gun Laws: Middle of the Road
Medical Marijuana: Yes
Recreational Marijuana: Legal

Colorado boasts some of the most beautiful mountains, flat and rolling plains, deserts, canyons, rivers, lakes, and forests in the US. It's no wonder the state is a haven for outdoor sport enthusiasts. The state is known for its world class ski resorts and the best skiing in the US.

As a result of all that outdoor exercise, people in Colorado have one of the lowest obesity rates in the US, despite also having a love of food and drink. Boulder is often named one of America's Foodiest Towns in recent years, and the town of Aspen's annual Food and Wine Classic is internationally known.

There are a quite a few microbreweries throughout the state, and together with macro breweries like Coors, Colorado produces more beer than any other state. Recreational use of Marijuana was approved in 2014 and can legally be bought from licensed businesses, possessed and used without fear of arrest or even a traffic ticket type civil fine. Medicinal marijuana has been an alternative to highly addictive prescription narcotics for treatment by doctors and their patients since 2000.

Did you know that Colorado has a higher chance of daily sunshine than even the "sunshine state" of Florida? If you'd like to retire among active healthy people in one of the most beautiful states in the US that offers a wide variety of world class four-season outdoor fun, Colorado may be your best bet. If you're an old hippie (or new) who'd like to smoke a joint occasionally, what are you waiting for? See a video of Colorado:

http://www.bestplacestoliveretire.com/2014/08/best-state-live-retire-colorado.html

Fort Collins, CO ***Grand Slam Town!

Fort Collins, a college town of 150,000 people, has made its way onto many best places lists in the last ten years. The population has grown significantly from 2000-2012, as people migrated to Fort Collins for its glorious scenery, abundant recreational opportunities and vibrant culture. Despite the growth, Fort Collins has been able to maintain its community spirit and small-town charm.

Fort Collins is home to the Colorado State University, which employs most of the city's residents. The town has a thriving restaurant, local live music and a micro-brew scene. Fort Collins is home to a cycling festival, many brewing events, car shows, and even a pro rodeo. The Colorado Marathon also takes place here, and it is considered the most scenic marathon in the nation.

Old Town in Fort Collins gives people a step back in time. You can visit a host of museums or take a tour through a part of town that is alive with culture and history. A very unique part of Fort Collins is the FC Bike Library. It is a free bicycle lending library, if you will, for locals, students, and visitors. You can borrow the bike for as long as you need, up to seven days.

Because Fort Collins is in Colorado, outdoor recreational opportunities are a must. The town has 50 parks and over 280 miles of trails for walking and biking, plus swimming pools, golf courses, ice rinks, whitewater rafting adventures, and of course hiking and fishing. You can truly find it all here, even hot air balloon rides and the nearby Rocky Mountain National Park. The beauty here cannot be matched as you enjoy any one of these outdoor activities.

Fort Collins is an amazing walkable, bike-able college and outdoor town. It's just a couple hours' drive from world-class skiing. If you want to live an active, healthy and fun-filled retirement, Fort Collins would be an excellent choice. The median sale price of homes here is about $250,000, which is just over the median for the state. See a video of Fort Collins:

http://www.bestplacestoliveretire.com/2014/08/best-town-to-live-or-retire-in-fort.html

More Top Towns in Colorado

Boulder*** Grand Slam Town! 100,000/$490,000
Carbondale (O) 6,500/$485,000
Fort Morgan (OV) 12,000/$129,000
Fruita (OV) 13,000/$220,000
Golden (C) 19,000/$335,000
Greely (C) 95,000/$167,000
Sterling (OV) 15,000/$99,000

Best State to Live in the US #3

70% Chance of Successful Long Term Relocation to Wyoming

Asset Protection: IRAs-A Non-IRA-F Homestead-D
Gun Laws: Strongly Favors Gun Owners
Medical Marijuana: No
Recreational Marijuana: Illegal

Wyoming is one of the least crowded and most rural states in the US. The state's capital, Cheyenne, is a smallish town of only 62,000 people, and it's also the most populated town in the state. Why should you at least consider Wyoming? Because a whopping 69% of Wyoming's residents feel the state is the best or at least one of the best states to live in. Only 46% of Florida's residents feel that way about their state, according to Gallup polling.

The reason Wyoming is our #3 pick is that it ranks higher in all quality of life factors than almost every other state. Wyoming does not have a personal state income tax, and the state sales tax is only 4%. Food is not subject to sales tax. Retirees with a fixed income and a tight budget can live better with tax policies like that. The state has some of the most business-friendly tax laws in the country too.

Grand Teton, Yellowstone, Devils Tower, Independence Rock, and Fossil Butte National Park are all in Wyoming. Jackson Hole, a world-class ski resort, is here too. This is an excellent place for biking, hiking, hunting, bird watching, fishing and really just about any outdoor activity or sport, all in a pristine environment.

If there's no way you would live in a crowded urban area and you desire a beautiful natural environment where you can breathe, Wyoming could be one of your best bets. See a video about Wyoming: http://www.bestplacestoliveretire.com/2014/08/best-state-retire-live-wyoming.html

Sheridan, WY

Looking for a small, friendly, outdoor town with lots community spirit? Sheridan, a town of only 17,700 with historic western charm and a mix of modern conveniences, could be just the place.

Sheridan has nine parks, including one with buffalo and elk and another with a beautiful fountain and ice skating. There are pathways for biking and walking located all through the city.

Some of what the residents do to enjoy all four seasons is hike, fish, hunt, golf, camp, horseback ride, and snowmobile. No matter the season, there is a reason to be outside taking in the fresh mountain air. While you do, you're likely to see big horn sheep, wild horses, deer, elk, and pheasants and more.

Sheridan has many festivals and events that draw in tourists and provide a better quality of life for locals. The 3rd Thursday Street Festival happens all summer and fills the streets with fun. There's Concerts in the Park, 1st People's Pow Wow, Winefest, and the Suds n' Spurs Brewfest. Whatever your flavor, they have an event for it! Of course, the big WYO Rodeo has been going strong for 84 years and is a major stop for all the pro cowboys and cowgirls.

There are many dining options in Sheridan, and the nightlife is hopping for such a small town. The Black Tooth Brewing Company and the Warehouse 201 are favorites for locals. Historic Main Street is always bustling with people shopping, eating, and meeting up with friends.

While many come here from smaller surrounding towns to visit, eat and shop, only the residents know the true happiness of living in such an intriguing and beautiful place. The median home price is around $200,000, slightly higher than Wyoming's median. See a video on Sheridan, Wyoming:

http://www.bestplacestoliveretire.com/2014/08/best-town-retire-live-sheridan.html

Top Wyoming Towns

Casper (OV) 56,000/$180,000
Gillette (OV) 30,000/$191,000
Lander (O) 8,000/$193,000
Laramie (C) 31,000/$191,000
Worland 6000/$125,000

Best States to Live in the US #2

75% Chance of Successful Long-Term Relocation to Montana

Asset Protection: IRAs-A NonIRA-F Homestead-C
Gun Laws: Strongly Favors Gun Owners
Medical Marijuana: Yes
Recreational Marijuana: Illegal

Montana offers a quality of life that is among the very best in the US. No other US state has higher resident satisfaction than Montana. Montana is the fourth largest state in the US, but is forty-fourth by population. Mountain ranges make up almost half of the state while the rest is prairie land. There are beautiful rock formations and very scenic badlands, as well as many lakes, rivers, and reservoirs. Glacier National Park, Little Bighorn Battlefield, and Yellowstone National Park are all in Montana.

Montana is a bountiful natural wonderland. Hiking, fishing, camping, golf, skiing, hunting and just about every other outdoor sport or activity is enjoyed here. The residents of Montana enjoy the outdoors all throughout four seasons. All that outdoor fun has led to Montana to being ranked as the least obese state in the U.S.

There is no sales tax in Montana. The state has college and outdoor towns. If you'd like to retire in a state that offers excellent outdoor recreational opportunities, a low crime rate, breathtaking scenery, a slower pace of life, then Montana is a state you'll want to consider. With a quality of life among the best in the US, together with the highest resident satisfaction, your chance of being happy with a move to Montana for retirement are high.

Bozeman, Montana*** A Grand Slam Town!

If you're looking for small-town atmosphere and a strong sense of community combined with the amenities of a much larger town, Bozeman, Montana might be the perfect place to retire for you. Bozeman is an amazing Rocky Mountains outdoor town near two world class ski areas, Big Sky and Bridger Bowl. It's also home to Montana State University.

Kayaking, backpacking, whitewater rafting, hiking, mountain biking, fishing and many other outdoor sports and activities are enjoyed in this four-season sport town and nearby Yellowstone Park. Downtown Bozeman is very pedestrian friendly, and there's plenty of shops, restaurants and bars to walk to. The town also offers residents art, culture and museum opportunities.

Located in a state with an exceptional quality of life and the highest resident satisfaction in the US, Bozeman may just be the best place to retire in the US, if winter sports or snowbirding will be part of your retirement plan. A college and outdoor town located in a state this highly rated in quality of life factors, means retirees moving here will have a high chance of a successful long-term satisfaction. Homes in this town of about 38,000 people have a median price of about $260,000.

Other Top Montana Towns

Butte-Silver Bow (OV) 31,000/$130,000
Dillon (C) 5,000/$139,000
Miles City (OV) 85,000/$94,000

The #1 Best State to Live in the US

75% Chance of Successful Long-Term Relocation to Utah

Asset Protection: IRAs-A NonIRA-F Homestead-D
Gun Laws: Strongly Favors Gun Owners
Medical Marijuana: No
Recreational Marijuana: Illegal

Utah has recently been named at or near the top of numerous "best states to live in" lists, including the #3 spot on Bankrates.com's excellent list of the best states to retire in. Utah ranked #2 in resident satisfaction. After looking at all the data, I've chosen Utah as the place that people moving for retirement will have the highest chance being happiest with their choice, long term.

Utah is yet another Rocky Mountain world-class outdoor recreation state with a low population density. The US Olympic Ski Team is headquartered here at one of Utah's world class ski resorts. Utah is gifted with seven national monuments, seven national forests and two national recreation areas.

Utah has the youngest population of any U.S. State, and it's also one of the fastest growing. Its economy is thriving. Many large corporations have made Utah their headquarters. Jobs, including high tech ones, are plentiful here. The state has a bright future economically and global warming-wise.

Utah's crime rate is one of the lowest in the US, and it rates high in all the important quality of life factors.

As a state, Utah may be the best overall choice for full-time retirement living, especially for those who will be enjoying winter sports as part of their retirement plan. It may also be the best choice for those who are going to become snowbirds and winter in places like nearby Arizona.

Provo, Utah*** A Grand Slam Town!

What's so special about Provo, Utah? Provo was named the best city to live in the US by Gallup. It has also been named best place for businesses, the happiest city, the best place to live and play, the most optimistic, and first in volunteerism.

Provo is a town of about 120,000 and home to Brigham Young University's 35,000 students. So yes, it's a college town. Like many other Rocky Mountain towns, it's also an outdoor recreation haven, but it's located in the #1 state for quality of life.

Provo is a bike and pedestrian friendly town with lots of shops and restaurants. The town hosts many festivals and has monthly art gallery strolls. There's an active nightlife here, even though there are only a few bars.

The median home value in Provo is about $220,000, which is about average for Utah. Provo is a world-class Rocky Mountain outdoor mecca and college town. Utah has a low crime rate, and Provo's rate is even lower. It certainly deserves its spot as one of the towns at the top of list of best places to retire.

Park City, Utah

If skiing and winter sports will a big part of your retirement plan, then Park City may be the best place in the US for you to retire. Park City has hosted the winter Olympics and is currently home to the U.S. Olympic Ski Team. Where else can you find a ski lift that whisks skiers from a historic downtown right to world class skiing?

Utah is a very conservative state, but Park City has the most active bar scene and nightlife in the state. There are plenty of upscale shops and fine dining in what was once an old mining town.

The Sundance Film Festival is held here every winter, as if the celebrities need more of a reason to flock to Park City than world-class skiing and nightlife. This is a town that truly worships winter.

Although Park City is as close as you can get to a perfect place to retire if you love winter sports, affordability is not its strong suit. The median cost of a home in Park City is over $700,000, 225% higher than Utah's average.

Other Top Utah Towns to Consider

Cedar City (C) 30,000/$190,000
Hurricane 15,000/$190,000
Logan (C) 50,000/$165,000
Roy 40,000/$160,000
South Ogden (O) 18,000/$180,000
Orem (C) 90,000/$210,000
St. George (O) 75,000/$230,000

#11- North Dakota

Chance of Successful Long-Term Relocation here 70%. Higher if you move here: Fargo, Grand Forks

Asset Protection: IRAs-C NonIRA-D Homestead-D
Gun Laws: Strongly Favors Gun Owners
Medical Marijuana: No
Recreational Marijuana: Illegal

#12- Idaho

Chance of Successful Long-Term Relocation here 60%. Higher if you move here: Boise, Idaho Falls, Moscow, Pocatello

Asset Protection: IRAs-A NonIRA-D Homestead-C
Gun Laws: Strongly Favors Gun Owners
Medical Marijuana: No
Recreational Marijuana: Illegal

#13- Iowa

Chance of Successful Long-Term Relocation here 60%. Higher if you move here: Ames, Iowa City

Asset Protection: IRAs-A NonIRA-F Homestead-A
Gun Laws: Middle of the Road
Medical Marijuana: No
Recreational Marijuana: Illegal

#14- Maine

Chance of Successful Long-Term Relocation here

60%. Higher if you move here: Augusta, Bangor, Brunswick, Old Orchard Beach, Portland

Asset Protection: IRAs-F Homestead-D Other-F
Gun Laws: Strongly Favors Gun Owners
Medical Marijuana: Yes
Recreational Marijuana: Decriminalized

#15- Virginia

Chance of Successful Long-Term Relocation here 55%. Higher if you move here: Blacksburg, Charlottesville, Chesapeake, Lynchburg

Asset Protection: IRAs-D Homestead-F Other-F
Gun Laws: Favors Gun Owners
Medical Marijuana: No
Recreational Marijuana: Illegal

#16- Washington

Chance of Successful Long-Term Relocation here 55%. Higher if you move here: Bellingham, Leavenworth

Asset Protection: IRAs-A Homestead-B Other-D
Gun Laws: Middle of the Road
Medical Marijuana: Yes
Recreational Marijuana: Legal

#17- Wisconsin

Chance of Successful Long-Term Relocation here 50%. Higher if you move here: Appleton, Eau Claire,

Madison, Menomonie, Oshkosh, Waukesha

Asset Protection: IRAs-D Homestead-D Other-C
Gun Laws: Middle of the Road
Medical Marijuana: No
Recreational Marijuana: Illegal

#18- Arizona

Chance of Successful Long-Term Relocation here 45%. Higher if you move here: Flagstaff, Prescott, Tempe, Tucson

Asset Protection: IRAs-A Homestead-B Other-A
Gun Laws: Strongly Favors Gun Owners
Medical Marijuana: Yes
Recreational Marijuana: Illegal

#19- Oklahoma

Chance of Successful Long-Term Relocation here 35%. Higher if you move here: Edmund, Norman, Tulsa

Asset Protection: IRAs-A Homestead-A Other-A
Gun Laws: Strongly Favors Gun Owners
Medical Marijuana: No
Recreational Marijuana: Illegal

#20- Massachusetts

Chance of Successful Long-Term Relocation here 45%. Higher if you move here: Boston, Cambridge, Northampton, Waltham

Asset Protection: IRAs-D Homestead-A Other-C
Gun Laws: Favors Gun Control
Medical Marijuana: Yes
Recreational Marijuana: Decriminalized

#21- Oregon

Chance of Successful Long-Term Relocation here 55%. Higher if you move here: Bend, Corvallis, Eugene, Klamath Falls, Portland, Roseburg, Salem

Gun Laws: Favors Gun Owners
Medical Marijuana: Yes
Recreational Marijuana: Decriminalized

#22- Georgia

Chance of Successful Long-Term Relocation here 40%. Higher if you move here: Athens, Elijay, Savanna, Valdosta

Asset Protection: IRAs-F Homestead-F Other-D
Gun Laws: Strongly Favors Gun Owners
Medical Marijuana: No
Recreational Marijuana: Illegal

#23- California

Chance of Successful Long-Term Relocation here 50%. Higher if you move here: Arcata, Irvine, Los Angles, Orange, Palo Alto, Petaloma, Redlands, San Francisco, San Luis Obispo, Santa Barbara, Santa Cruz

Asset Protection: IRAs-F Homestead-D Other-D

Gun Laws: Strongly Favors Gun Control
Medical Marijuana: Yes
Recreational Marijuana: Decriminalized

#24- Alaska

Chance of Successful Long-Term Relocation here 70% . Higher if you move here: Fairbanks

Asset Protection: IRAs-A Homestead-D Other-F
Gun Laws: Strongly Favors Gun Owners
Medical Marijuana: Yes
Recreational Marijuana: Decriminalized

#25-Hawaii

Chance of Successful Long-Term Relocation here 65%. No Picks

Asset Protection: IRAs-B Homestead-F Other-A
Gun Laws: Favors Gun Control
Medical Marijuana: Yes
Recreational Marijuana: Illegal

#26- Kansas

Chance of Successful Long-Term Relocation here 40%. Higher if you move here: Lawrence, Manhattan, Overland Park

Asset Protection: IRAs-F Homestead-A Other-A
Gun Laws: Strongly Favors Gun Owners
Medical Marijuana: No
Recreational Marijuana: Illegal

#27- Tennessee

Chance of Successful Long-Term Relocation here 45%. Higher if you move here: Cookeville, Knoxville, Murfreesboro, Nashville

Asset Protection: IRAs-B Homestead-F Other-F
Gun Laws: Strongly Favors Gun Owners
Medical Marijuana: No
Recreational Marijuana: Illegal

#28- Nevada

Chance of Successful Long-Term Relocation here 35%. Higher if you move here: Reno

Asset Protection: IRAs-B Homestead-B Other-D
Gun Laws: Strongly Favors Gun Owners
Medical Marijuana: Yes
Recreational Marijuana: Decriminalized (over age 21)

#29- Pennsylvania

Chance of Successful Long-Term Relocation here 40%. Higher if you move here: Altoona, Bethlehem, Carlisle, Greensburg, Jim Thorpe, Kutztown, Lancaster, Meadville, State College, West Chester

Asset Protection: IRAs-C Homestead-F Other-F
Gun Laws: Middle of the Road
Medical Marijuana: No
Recreational Marijuana: Illegal

#30-Delaware

Chance of Successful Long-Term Relocation here 40%. Higher if you move here: Smyrna

Asset Protection: IRAs-A Homestead-D Other-F
Gun Laws: Favors Gun Control
Medical Marijuana: Yes
Recreational Marijuana: Illegal

#31- Florida

Chance of Successful Long-Term Relocation here 40%. Higher if you move here: Dunedin Englewood/Rotonda, Gainesville, Safety Harbor, Venice, Weston

Asset Protection: IRAs-A Homestead-A Other-A
Gun Laws: Strongly Favors Gun Owners
Medical Marijuana: No
Recreational Marijuana: Illegal

#32- South Carolina

Chance of Successful Long-Term Relocation here 40%. Higher if you move here: Charleston, Clemson

Asset Protection: IRAs-F Homestead-D Other-F
Gun Laws: Strongly Favors Gun Owners
Medical Marijuana:
Recreational Marijuana:

#33- North Carolina

Chance of Successful Long-Term Relocation here

...igher if you move here: Apex, Banner Elk, Boone, Chapel Hill, Davidson

Asset Protection: IRAs-A Homestead-F Other-C
Gun Laws: Strongly Favors Gun Owners
Medical Marijuana: No
Recreational Marijuana: Illegal

#34- New Mexico

Chance of Successful Long-Term Relocation here 35%. Higher if you move here: Los Alamos

Asset Protection: IRAs-A Homestead-C Other-A
Gun Laws: Strongly Favors Gun Owners
Medical Marijuana: Yes
Recreational Marijuana: Illegal

#35 Missouri

Chance of Successful Long-Term Relocation here 35%. Higher if you move here: Chesterfield, Lee's Summit, Warrensburg

Asset Protection: IRAs-F Homestead-F Other-D
Gun Laws: Strongly Favors Gun Owners
Medical Marijuana: No
Recreational Marijuana: Illegal

#36- Indiana

Chance of Successful Long-Term Relocation here 35%. Higher if you move here: Bloomington, Noblesville, Valparaiso, West Lafayette

Asset Protection: IRAs-A Homestead-F Other-F
Gun Laws: Favors Gun Owners
Medical Marijuana: No
Recreational Marijuana: Illegal

#37- Kentucky

Chance of Successful Long-Term Relocation here 35%. Higher if you move here: Bardstown, Lexington, Murray

Asset Protection: IRAs-A Homestead-F Other-D
Gun Laws: Strongly Favors Gun Owners
Medical Marijuana: No
Recreational Marijuana: Illegal

#38- Alabama

Chance of Successful Long-Term Relocation here 35%. Higher if you move here: Auburn, Vestavia Hills
Asset Protection: IRAs-F Homestead-F Other-D
Gun Laws: Favors Gun Owners
Medical Marijuana: No
Recreational Marijuana: Illegal

#39- Illinois

Chance of Successful Long-Term Relocation here 25%. Higher if you move here: Crystal Lake, Edwardsville

Asset Protection: IRAs-A Homestead-F Other-C
Gun Laws: Favors Gun Control
Medical Marijuana: No

Recreational Marijuana: Illegal

#40- New York

Chance of Successful Long-Term Relocation here 35%. Higher if you move here: Geneseo, Ithica, Oneonta, Potsdam, New Paltz, Saratoga Springs

Asset Protection: IRAs-A Homestead-D Other-C
Gun Laws: Strongly Favors Gun Control
Medical Marijuana: Yes
Recreational Marijuana: Decriminalized (unless used in public view)

#41- Michigan

Chance of Successful Long-Term Relocation here 35%. Higher if you move here: Ann Arbor, Kalamazoo, Mount Pleasant, Traverse City

Asset Protection: IRAs-B Homestead-D Other-A
Gun Laws: Middle of the Road
Medical Marijuana: Yes
Recreational Marijuana: Illegal

#42- Ohio

Chance of Successful Long-Term Relocation here 35%. Higher if you move here:Bowling Green, Delaware, Granville, Kent, Marietta, Wiberforce

Asset Protection: IRAs-F Homestead-F Other-D
Gun Laws: Favors Gun Owners
Medical Marijuana: Yes

Recreational Marijuana: Illegal

43- Rhode Island

Chance of Successful Long-Term Relocation here 25%. Higher if you move here:Kingston, Newport

Asset Protection: IRAs-A Homestead-B Other-D
Gun Laws: Favors Gun Control
Medical Marijuana: Yes
Recreational Marijuana: Decriminalized

#44- Arkansas

Chance of Successful Long-Term Relocation here 35%. Higher if you move here:Conway, Fayetteville, Mountain View, Russelville, Searcy

Asset Protection: IRAs-F Homestead-C Other-F
Gun Laws: Strongly Favors Gun Owners
Medical Marijuana: No
Recreational Marijuana: Illegal

#45- West Virginia

Chance of Successful Long-Term Relocation here 35%. Higher if you move here:Fayetteville, Huntington, Morgantown

Asset Protection: IRAs-F Homestead-F Other-F
Gun Laws: Strongly Favors Gun Owners
Medical Marijuana: No
Recreational Marijuana: Illegal

#46- New Jersey

Chance of Successful Long-Term Relocation here 25%. Higher if you move here: Ewing, Glassboro, Madison, Princeton, West Long Branch

Asset Protection: IRAs-A Homestead-F Other-F
Gun Laws: Strongly Favors Gun Control
Medical Marijuana: Yes
Recreational Marijuana: Illegal

#47- Connecticut

Chance of Successful Long-Term Relocation here 35%. Higher if you move here: Middletown, Mystic, Willimantic

Asset Protection: IRAs-A Homestead-C Other-F
Gun Laws: Strongly Favors Gun Control
Medical Marijuana: Yes
Recreational Marijuana: Decriminalized (unless near a school or daycare)

#48- Mississippi

Chance of Successful Long-Term Relocation here 25%. Higher if you move here: Hattiesburg, Starkville

Asset Protection: IRAs-A Homestead-C Other-F
Gun Laws: Strongly Favors Gun Owners
Medical Marijuana: No
Recreational Marijuana: Decriminalized (first offence only)

#49- Maryland

Asset Protection: IRAs-A Homestead-F Other-A
Chance of Successful Long-Term Relocation here 30%. Higher if you move here: Annapolis, Frederick, Towson

Gun Laws: Strongly Favors Gun Control
Medical Marijuana: Yes
Recreational Marijuana: Decriminalized

#50- Louisiana

Chance of Successful Long-Term Relocation here 25%. Higher if you move here: Grambling

Asset Protection: IRAs-B Homestead-D Other-D
Gun Laws: Strongly Favors Gun Owners
Medical Marijuana: No
Recreational Marijuana: Illegal

Summary and Tips

- Selling your home and right-sizing for retirement, especially if you can cash in on the tax free home profit exclusion, may be a good move for many retirees.
- The best places to move for retirement for most people will be to a home with as little maintenance and as few steps as possible, or one that is easily made handicap accessible (just in case). These types of homes will probably increase in value and sell faster in a future when more senior buyers are in the

market.

- Retiring in place or within a four-hour drive (less than 1 hour preferable) where you still have family and social ties may be best for many retirees.
- When moving for retirement, a college town or outdoor recreation town (find a town that's both and you have it made) that is pedestrian and bike friendly with a vibrant downtown would be an excellent choice for most retirees.
- Making a long distance move to enjoy retirement can be expensive and risky. Thorough research, moving to a town you already have family living in, and moving to a state with higher resident satisfaction, all lower your risk.
- Use caution when your main reason for moving is you're tired of the cold or shoveling snow. Explore options discussed later in this book to mitigate that problem, such a snowbirding. Too many moves to "warmer" locations turn out to be an expensive mistake that can be corrected only by losing more time and money.

Making a Great Choice Better

Still the Most Popular Choice

Despite daydreams of how wonderful moving to some tropical location for retirement would be, retiring in place is what most retirees still do. That is the least risky choice and probably the wisest choice for most retirees. Keep the tropical island as a place to visit on vacation or snowbird in, but not to live full time.

The Reasons it's Popular

One of the main reasons people regret moving for retirement is that they underestimate or don't even consider the effect being separated from family and long-term friends will have on them. Being connected to others is essential for our health and well-being; it's hardwired into us. Retiring in place means we don't separate ourselves from the packs we already are a part of, so we can spend our energy on building new groups and pursuits to replace those of our old workplace, as covered latter in the book.

Most long distance moves mean having to start from scratch just to build your first connection in your new home. No matter what you do, you can't create family or long-term friends. Finding a new doctor or dentist in a brand new place that you'll like, or least be comfortable with, can be very challenging. Trying to find a barber or hairstylist that can cut your hair the way you like can be difficult. Most people don't realize how much time, money, energy and aggravation they save by retiring in place.

Moving for Retirement but Staying Local

Is the home you're living in the right size for your retirement life? Would saving on rent or real estate taxes, insurance, heating and cooling costs help you reduce anxiety and stress? Could saving money on housing help fund the better retirement you really want?

There are many advantages to living in the perfect size home for your next stage of life, if you are now paying for space you don't use. Do you really want to do more cleaning, grass cutting and snow shoveling than you have to?

In the past you may have had to sell your home at a less than optimal time because of job promotion in another state, the loss of a job, or for more space after the birth of a child. You have an advantage now if you're retired or planning for it because you can wait to sell when the market is high to put the most cash in your pocket.

Depending upon where you live, this can be terrific financial move. Are there areas within an hour of where you now live that have lower home prices? Usually within an hour of most cities or suburbs there are smaller towns or even vacation wilderness areas near lakes or the mountains, with beautiful homes at lower prices. Along with lower home prices in these areas, you can often get lower taxes, less traffic, lower stress and a higher quality of life.

In many mountain or lake communities where cabins or vacation type homes are common, the lot is fully wooded except the driveway and a walkway, so there's no grass to cut or lawn mower to own and replace every few years. What would you rather be doing, cutting grass or hiking with new friends to the top of a mountain for a picnic complete with wine?

Are there small towns that are more bike or pedestrian friendly within an hour or two of where you now live with single unattached homes that have very little yard? You could landscape a small yard with plants, shrubs, flowers, walkways and sitting areas, ending up with no grass to cut. Are there any safe small towns nearby with lower housing costs where you could walk to restaurants, grocery stores restaurants and pubs? That could save you money on gas and auto insurance by allowing you to drive fewer miles and out of the city. The walking could improve your health and weight, and small town life can lower your stress level.

It doesn't cost anything to examine your housing needs to see if a move to another community makes sense. A friendly small town close enough to your family, friends and doctor so that you could easily travel there any day you please would be ideal. Maybe a right-size in the town where you now live would be a good idea. The key here is to see if there are homes that will cost less to live in, but still meet your needs, require less maintenance and be close enough to your family and friends that you won't feel disconnected.

Selling Your Home and Reaping Tax Free Profit

If you're a homeowner, you may qualify for the IRS's home sales tax exclusion. This gift from the IRS allows you to sell your home and pocket the profit between what you paid and what you sell for, tax free, if you qualify. Taking advantage of this gift from the IRS may help you buy a right-size home and put money in the bank. It could also help you take advantage of other retirement options mentioned in this book, like snowbirding.

Given the federal government's budget problems, there's no guarantee the law allowing no tax on home sales gains won't disappear. So why not take advantage of it now while you can, if selling and buying better would be right for you? Besides, if you do a buy another home, the clock starts again and you may be able to do it again in the future if the law doesn't change.

Maybe there are other retirement lifestyle options in this book that you would love, but thought you couldn't afford, like buying an RV and traveling to warmer climates in the winter and cooler ones in the summer. Selling, cashing in and right-sizing could be the perfect move to allow you to enjoy the retirement you didn't think you could afford, but always wanted.

How to Winter

If retiring in place is the best decision for you, but you have concerns about winter, here's a few suggestions if snowbirding and other options aren't right for you all year round, including winter.

Some Tips

- Get free window treatment and color ideas by visiting higher-end model homes of larger builders. Take a small notepad and pen along and write down in detail anything you think might work well in your home.
- Consider painting your walls and ceilings white. For some color, consider the lightest shades of colors on any swatch.
- Consider using a semi-gloss paint on the walls. It will reflect some light and brighten the room without looking cheap as a high gloss paint might. Semi-gloss walls are easier to clean than walls painted with a flat paint.
- Consider vertical wood blinds or curtains that will expose nearly the whole window when open to allow lots of light into the home.

Winter and Fire

Having dinner, a drink or just watching TV is just better when done in a room with the ambiance of a glowing fire. If you haven't seen some of the newer fireplaces and wood stoves, you'll be amazed at the thousands of styles now available. Prices start in the $100's, but you can easily spend $1000's. It's an investment that could increase the value and salability of your home, put you in a better mood all winter, and pay for itself in lower heating costs.

Winter Soaks

Most accommodations in winter resorts areas have hot tubs for use by their guests. There's nothing better than a good soak after a day of winter exercise. Many cabins on the slopes have the hot tub just outside on the deck. There's something exhilarating about being in 100+ degree bubbling water massaging your body while looking up at a star-filled night sky. If you're going to be wintering at home, you may want to consider getting a hot tub or spa. After a soak and a shower, you'll feel years younger. If you have certain medical conditions, a doctor's prescription could make a hot tub purchase a medical tax deduction. Consult your doctor and or tax professional to see if you qualify.

Consider buying in the summer when retailers may be persuaded to sell for a lower price. That would be the ideal time to install some shrubs for privacy too. While unenlightened people dread the approach of winter, you may actually look forward to nightly dinners by the fireplace and soothing soaks.

Outdoor Fire and Furniture

There are some amazing options available today that can transform a deck, patio or other outside area into a living-room under the stars. Outdoor furniture, gas fire-pit tables and gas heaters can allow you to extend the period of time you can enjoy the outside areas of your home, and you may be able to do so for less than you imagined.

One idea is to right-size your home to actual needs, pocket the tax-free profit, and use a few thousand dollars to invest in making your home live larger, by putting together an outdoor area that will be the envy of your friends. Of course, if you invite them over for an outdoor dinner and drinks, followed by a soothing soak while looking at city lights or a star-filled sky while all the neighbors are inside, they'll surely be thankful.

Tired of Shoveling Snow

While I was selling homes in Florida, you would not believe how many people told me they were moving to Florida because they were tired of shoveling snow. Sometimes just for fun I would ask them why they didn't just buy a snow-blower. The answer I got most often? "You kidding? They're way too expensive." An $800 snowblower is too expensive, but spending $50,000-$100,000 or more to move somewhere "warmer" isn't?

No one moving to Florida ever told me they were tired of using their snow-blower. Snow-blowers can be like a best friend when retiring in place. If winter and shoveling snow is your main reason for leaving an area where you have friends, family and other ties, you may want to learn about new technology that makes snowblowers safer and easier to use, or consider becoming a snowbird.

Snow and Ice No More

If you have some extra cash and you want a snow and ice-free driveway without any hassle, you may want to have a system installed where all you have to do is flip a switch.

For videos and more helpful retire-in-place resources go to:

http://www.bestplacestoliveretire.com/2015/02/r etire-place-resourses.html

Retirement Just Your New Job

Anatole France (1844-1924), French poet, journalist and author, once said "We must die to one life before we can enter another." Wow. So retiring means our old work life must die so our new life can begin? No wonder some fear retirement so much that they won't stop working. Great news—no one has to fear retiring anymore because we're all just going to start a new job, retirement.

New Job Slacking Allowed

Like all new jobs, you'll be taking on new responsibilities and challenges, but you've done that before, so no problem there. In your new job you will not have a support staff, title, name badge or specific role you must play. The upside is, now that you don't have any specific role you must play, you can really just be yourself, maybe for the first time since you were a kid.

In your new job, you're allowed to work from home or anywhere in the world you want to. You are completely free to make your own schedule as long as you fulfill your responsibilities. If you use your time wisely, you will be richly rewarded. If you waste time or slack off, you'll suffer the consequences, much like your last job.

Responsibilities of Your New Job

At your old job you were part of a pack, a tribe, a community that worked together in a modern version of hunting and gathering, just as your ancestors did for millions of years. That's why even if you constantly complained about your job, you may actually miss the old pack you've been a part of for many years, even the people you really didn't like.

Don't fear separation from the people at work because your new job permits you to join a new pack, or many of them if that's what you desire to do. Actually, the first responsibility of your new job is to find new packs to modern-day hunt and gather with, whether that means biking mountain trails, spinning class, quilting or whatever you really want to do with your retirement. If you're not sure, that's OK because you'll find some ideas coming up shortly.

The great thing about your new job is that you will get to choose the packs you want to become part of. If you're passionate about something or want to pursue a particular activity, you're free to join packs, tribes or communities of people that feel the same way. Are you starting to see how much better your new job is going to be compared to your old one?

Replacing the old pack at work is important because studies have shown that belonging to a community is a common trait among the people who enjoy the longest and healthiest lives. Other studies show that becoming a lone wolf increases the risk of depression, disease and premature death. Joining new packs will not only be fun and exciting—it's actually very healthy physically and mentally and can help you live longer.

Hunt and Gather with Your Pack

Your wonderful new job's second responsibility is to maintain and improve your health. That's why joining packs with pursuits that involve physical activity are excellent choices. When your new pack starts to hunt and gather (hike, bike, garden, etc.), you can participate and move along with them. If not, your chances of survival plummet. You're a predator's dream if you're just sitting there motionless on the couch by yourself while your pack is out hunting and gathering. Why? Because hunting and gathering requires exercising that terrific body you were given.

You were given an amazing body free and clear. It's the result of millions of years of development and evolution. It's incredibly capable and will work great for you . . . if you keep it maintained. If you fail to maintain it and it starts to break down, you can't trade it for a new one as if it were a car.

Better Health Equals More Fun

Your amazing body was built for about 10 hours of

hunting and gathering a day because that's what was required of it for a million years just to survive. Luckily, you don't have to hunt and gather all day to survive any more, but because the body you have was designed for that, some activity every day will keep it in good working order. You can get away with the equivalent of about one hour of low aerobic activity a day.

How to Exercise Without Working Out

One hour of activity doesn't have to be exercise, but it certainly could be if there are some forms of it you enjoy, like biking. Many of us hate the idea of exercise, and that's why we're going to find stuff we love to do, that we'll just happen to get exercise while doing. The Blue Zone studies showed that the people who lived the longest healthiest lives on the planet don't even own exercise equipment or belong to a gym. Their lifestyle has low impact aerobic activities built right into it. They live in areas where they walk to shops, visit with family and friends, and tend their gardens.

If you move to a town where you can walk to almost everywhere you need to go, you can get your one hour's worth of exercise without planning or even thinking about it. Many of this book's recommendations for the best places to retire are college or outdoor towns (the absolute best places are both) that are very pedestrian or bike friendly. Imagine getting a new job requiring one hour of activity just by going about your day with no "exercising."

If you're going to move for retirement anyway, why

not choose a place where you can walk or bike to a great restaurant, grocery store or friendly neighborhood pub or almost everywhere you have to go? Living in the boring burbs where you must get in your car to go anywhere or do anything is so 1970s. Why risk a DUI just for having a couple of drinks with dinner? Walk to and from a friendly neighborhood dinning establishment in a safe town. Such places really still exist.

Living in such a place, you'll likely become friends with some of the shopkeepers and patrons. It'll be easier to meet and get to know your neighbors. You could be fulfilling two of the three requirements of your new job, joining new packs or communities and exercising, just by doing what you would do every day anyway.

The Whole Point

The third responsibility of your new job is to enjoy having fun and don't waste time. The main difference between your old job and your new one is that your role in your old job was to do was best for your boss, the company, or your kids. Guess what? Now it's time to do what *you* want. It's time to do what's best for you. After 50, 60 or 70 years, it's finally your turn to come first.

This may not be easy, at first. The habit you've built and nurtured of putting others and your responsibilities to others first and foremost is not going to be easy to break. This is not about becoming selfish: It's just about realizing that you have reached a time in your life that where you are no longer responsible for the same things you were for decades. The weight has been lifted from your shoulders.

You may experience feelings of guilt just at the thought of putting yourself first. Acknowledge the feeling of guilt if it happens and decide if it's justified or not. If it isn't, if it's just part of the 50-year habit you had, then drop it and move on with planning what you want to do now that you are finally free, freer than any time since you were a kid and your parents took care of all the problems.

On Wasting Time

Do you know how much time you have left on this planet? I mean, do you know if you have 10 years, 20 or maybe 30 years left on earth? Don't worry, nobody really knows for sure, of course. What is for sure, is that there is a number. For instance, let's say the number is 20 years, just as an example. In this example, we only have 20 years of life left to enjoy.

Since we only have 20 years left, every hour takes us closer to our expiration date. Every second that clock ticks means we have used one second of our limited time. So if we waste an hour of our time, we've also wasted an hour of our life. So wasting time means wasting life. The third responsibility of our new job is to have fun and don't waste time.

Summary and Tips

- Your new job requires that you find new friends and communities to replace the old ones you had at your last job. These new people will improve your life because you'll choose people who share your interests and passions. Your new job will also allow you the freedom to spend more time with family and friends you enjoy.

- Your new job requires that you actively take care of the only body you have. You'll find ways to accomplish this doing things you absolutely love.
- Your new job requires that you have fun and enjoy life. You can accomplish this by making sure that you are always researching, planning or doing something you truly enjoy. When in doubt, ask yourself "Is this the most enjoyable activity I can realistically be doing right now?"

Your Funtirement Plan

The great thing about your new job is that you and your spouse or significant other if you have one, have full control over your new job schedule. You get to decide what adventurous and exciting activities will fill your days and where you'll be pursuing them. You can accomplish this through a retirement plan that has absolutely nothing to do with putting money away or investing.

Here's an example of a funtirement plan. This retired couple have decided to live the overseas living travel lifestyle covered in a previous chapter. They'll live in furnished apartments or homes overseas in different locations for three-month periods of time while also running a very part-time business that can be operated from any location that has an internet connection because it is an online business (also discussed later):

- We'll downsize to a small, friendly, safe, walkable but active town close to our current one. The home will better meet our needs in this stage of our life and will be much more affordable. We'll bank the tax-free profit difference between what we got for our old home and what we paid cash for the new one and keep it as a large emergency fund.
- We'll travel to and live in beautiful, safe overseas countries that we can afford to live in on just our fixed retirement income. We'll stay in rented furnished homes or apartments.
- We'll wake up each morning and work at our own pace, on our own business for a couple of hours. We'll skip this on days we have other things planned for that morning. Our choice of retirement income generation will allow us to work from anywhere in the world that has internet service. We might be doing it from an office in our home or while we're admiring the view of a vineyard in France.
- In the afternoon we'll bike, hike, ski or sight see so we can get the exercise we need to be our healthiest while enjoying something we both love to do.
- In the evening we'll will either cook a delicious nutritious meal and enjoy some red wine or we'll walk into town and enjoy good food and drink at an outdoor table when the weather is nice or inside by a fireplace when snow's on the ground.

- In order to keep this lifestyle from getting anywhere close to monotonous, the location where we'll wake up in the morning will never be the same all year long. We'll travel to different locations we've always wanted to visit for one-to-three-month periods to learn more about the culture, people and language, if different from our own.

How's that for a retirement plan? As you can see, a plan for how to use the gift of time your new job provides you doesn't have to be complicated. Here's another plan. This example is what a plan for a single woman who would like to meet new people and socialize might look like:

- I'll spend many of my mornings volunteering because after reading "How to Retire Happier," I realized I've always donated money to causes, but I never donated my time. So before I retired, I tested volunteering out. I learned after 65 years that when I give my time, I actually benefit more than the people I help. I feel better about myself and my role in the world after giving back, and some of the other volunteers have become very good friends. Volunteering and helping others will become a permanent part of my retirement life.
- On the mornings I don't volunteer, I'll take care of chores around the house, grocery shopping, etc.
- Most afternoons I'll participate in a scheduled ride with the bike club I joined through the bike shop where I bought my wonderful new bike. I

never would have thought that I'd take up biking again at age 65. I've already joined a ski club that my new bike friends belong to because that's what they do in winter. I look forward to learning how to ski. I'm amazed at how many retirees are getting involved in these types of pursuits today.

- I'll continue going out to movies, dinners and dancing and otherwise socializing with my new friends from the bike club whenever I feel up to it; they always seem to have something going on.

- It seems that I'm always on the go, but I love it. I'm doing great with my new job responsibilities (retirement) because I'm getting more exercise now that I ever have, and I feel great. I've also have a whole new set of people that I see almost every day, and they're a lot more fun than the people at work ever were. I would have retired sooner if I had known this was how it was going to be.

What's that? You say that you could never enjoy a life like that because . . . . Stop right there. Today's new retirees are participating in sports of all kinds that they never dreamed they would—and loving it. They are joining groups of active, healthy, fun loving people who are enjoying life more now than they ever have in the past. So why can't you?

Newly retired singles and couples are traveling and seeing sites that they've always dreamed about. They're camping out in nature under star-filled skies, some in RV's and others in tents. They're hiking, biking and learning how to ski and loving it. So why can't you?

Is enjoying an amazing life after retirement only for other people? Is excitement, adventure and joy only for other people? Of course not! That's ridiculous! You've worked hard all your life (mostly). You sacrificed for your job, your boss and your kids. You played by the rules, put others' needs before yours and took care of all of your responsibilities the best you could.

You've now reached that time you were told to save for. You denied many wants and desires because you were promised that someday you would be able to retire. So now you're there, or soon will be, so why not you? The truth is, there is absolutely no reason why you can't live the adventurous, exciting life you deserve from now on. It will just require a little effort to get started—and a plan.

Planning a Lifetime Vacation

Have you ever planned a vacation? Of course you have, and you loved it. Why? Because you did your homework and planned it. You didn't just get in the car without a map, reservations, tickets or plan and just start driving.

It's the same thing with retirement. You're just planning a very, very long vacation. Just as planning your vacation leads to having a good time, so will planning your retirement. The best part? Planning is easier and more fun because you don't have to fit it all into just a week so you can be back at work.

Making Your Plan

So how do you plan this new vacation? First, let's identify what needs, wants and desires we might have that could become part of a plan. Every morning, get out a piece of paper first thing, maybe with a cup of coffee, and write "What would I most like to be doing right now if money were no object?" at the top of it. Then write down everything and anything that comes to mind. Don't hold back: Write everything that comes to mind even if you think there's no way that it could ever happen or that you'll be able to afford it.

On another piece of paper, write "Where would I rather be right now, if money weren't an object?" Again, write down everything that you can think of. Do this every morning for a few days. This little exercise will help draw out your true desires.

Some of us will have no problem coming up with a list. For others, it may be hard to think of anything at all because your wants and needs were suppressed for decades in order to take care of responsibilities. Don't worry about that. As you read further, you'll find ideas for adventurous pursuits that may work for you. You won't need the list until the end of the book anyway. So relax.

You May Love This if You Tried it

Please do not skip paragraphs in this because you see a heading and think "there's no way I'm doing that" Reading about a pursuit may spark an emotion that could lead you finding something that you passionately love to do, but never would have even tried, if you hadn't read that one sentence that took only a second to do.

Many of the following activities by themselves may help you meet all of the requirements of your new job. They may lead you to join a new group of people. You may exercise your body while enjoying the activity, and you may also have an amazingly great time.

It Could Happen to You Too

After reading about how much fun new bikes are, thanks to technology, what if you forced yourself to take a free test ride? What if you loved it? You may buy an amazing new bike that you love to ride because even the slightest effort from you propels the bike forward. You may love it so much that you ride almost every day, so you're meeting the first responsibility of your new job, taking care of your body with a minimum one hour of low-intensity aerobic daily.

Maybe you also forced yourself to go on a group starter ride the bike shop sponsored, even though you "knew" you hated that kind of stuff, but instead, you had the time of your life. You also met some great new people, and you really don't like people. What if some of them turned into good friends and now you ride with them and socialize afterwards almost daily? You would meet your second responsibility of finding a new pack that replaces those jerks at work. You're having a great time, so you've covered the last responsibility too, all from getting involved in one activity that you haven't done for 35 years and thought you'd absolutely hate.

The moral? Even if you see the heading and think "there's no way," it won't take much time, and if you don't, you may miss out on something that could turn into a pursuit you'll surprisingly love, one that can help you live a longer, healthier life.

Recommended Core Activities

Activities or pursuits that can be very beneficial and enjoyed by almost all retirees regardless of age are highlighted by ***. These are activities that should be a part of almost every retiree's retirement plan. They can be a core daily activity or just a fill-in for days when you can't do your other chosen pursuits.

So Natural*** Recommended Core Activity

Walking is an activity that should be a part of almost every modern retiree's retirement plan. It's what our ancestors did for hours a day, every day, for millions of years. It's what your body is designed and built for. It's one of the cheapest possible activities you can do, and you can do it by yourself, with your significant other if you have one, or with a pack.

If you aren't already an avid walker, you may be surprised just how many aesthetically interesting paths and trails there are to explore in just about every town in this country today. Some areas have gone all out and developed so many miles of walking and biking paths that you could explore a different trail and enjoy different scenery every day of the week, or for a month in some areas.

A good pair of walking shoes that cost about $60 or less from a specialty footwear or sporting goods store is recommended, but just about any pair of sneakers will get you started. New technology makes walking longer distances more comfortable in actual "walking shoes."

Even the best walking shoes are cheap compared to the payoff of better health and well-being they'll bring you. Walking is a pursuit that just about anyone at any age can do and benefit from. This should be a core pursuit for just about every "person of leisure." Once you make the small investment in a comfortable pair of walking shoes, the trails and bike paths are free. Even if you've saved absolutely nothing for your retirement, you can easily afford this free beneficial activity.

In my opinion, walking on a treadmill inside a home or gym is boring, something that only hamsters should do. I'd rather stick hangers in my ears than walk on a treadmill. A study done in 2009 published by "Medicine & Science in Sports & Exercise" found that people will exercise longer when they are outside compared to exercising at home or in a gym. Breathing outdoor air is healthier than indoor air, unless you live in Beijing. However, if you like using a treadmill indoors or at a gym, I envy you.

If you're considering a move for retirement, moving to a pedestrian-friendly town where you walk to shopping, restaurants and bars is a great way to walk for health without even having to think about it. Living in such communities is a common factor among people who live the longest, healthiest lives on earth, according to the Blue Zone and other studies.

Getting a pedometer, a small device that you wear that counts how many steps you're walking every day, can be useful.

You can see videos about walking, walking clubs or how to start one, walking trail maps, tips and more at:
http://www.bestplacestoliveretire.com/2015/02/walking-core-healthy-retirement-activity.html

In Nature*** Recommended Core Activity

This is just walking, but usually in more adventurous places. Hiking is a walk to a mountain peak where your can see for hundreds of miles, or to a beautiful hidden waterfall landscape. Like walking, this is a pursuit that almost everyone can do and afford to enjoy. Hiking is a pursuit that's best done with a partner or group. Singles can usually find a club that will be glad to share their love of hiking, and it'll be a way to meet new people. Getting in shape, getting healthier, losing weight and socializing while breathing fresh outdoor air—how great is that?

Living in areas with lots of parks and or mountain trails to explore can add many benefits to your life. Outdoor exercise and breathing clean air does wonders for the body. You may feel better physically and mentally and enjoy sleep better, as many hikers report.

You may see a lot of wildlife, including interesting, colorful birds on your hikes. That may lead you to want to get binoculars to better see the wildlife or that peak of the next mountain close up. That may spark an interest in getting books on bird watching or rocks and plant identification.

Hiking may lead to a desire to photograph what you see and have large prints of your best shots made to frame and hang on the walls of your home. You may even end up selling your "work" online or through local retailers. Who knows, you may buy an RV and travel south for the winter, paying for your adventures by selling your work at the many art and craft festivals or flea markets that are held in snow-birding places like Florida and Arizona during the winter months.

The possibilities for expanding your interests and enjoyment are enormous with just a little effort to get out there and try new things. What if you really have an undiscovered talent for outdoor photography that could finance travel to all the places you want to see, but you never discover it because you didn't take that first hike?

Retirement is a time to explore. Resist the negative thoughts that try to convince you that you won't like something before you really give it a shot. Buy some hiking shoes from a store that has a 100% no-questions-asked guarantee and take a short hike to a place that promises to offer a great experience or view. If you find you love it, great! Once you buy the hiking boots, the trails are free. Even if you didn't save a nickle for retirement, you can afford free.

Your inherited an amazing body and mind from your ancestors that was built to walk with others, especially in nature. What a perfect match hiking is.

http://www.bestplacestoliveretire.com/2015/02/hiking-health-core-retirement-pursuit.html

It's Even More Fun Now*** Recommended Core Activity

If it's been years since you've been on a bike, you're missing out. The bikes found today in bike specialty shops are lighter and faster, and even a small amount of effort will propel you farther than the bikes you grew up with.

Biking is a no-impact, healthy sport that you can enjoy at almost any age. They even have three wheeled bikes that are light, fast and even look cool. These are definitely not your grandmother's clunky, heavy old trike.

Biking has become so popular among healthy retirees you can find welcoming bike clubs just about anywhere. Many people love belonging to a bike club because they have regular group rides scheduled almost daily that often begin and end socializing at a cafe or pub.

The best bike brands are sold only through bike specialty shops because that's where you'll find people qualified to properly fit and set up your bike for maximum safety and enjoyment. Expect to pay at least $500 for a good bike (*Consumer Reports* says the cheap bikes sold at big box stores can actually be dangerous.) Hot-looking, fast three wheelers cost a little more.

Trust me, the extra cost of a good bike can mean the difference between discovering an exciting sport you'll love for the rest of your life, or sitting on the couch with a cheap, heavy, clunky bike sitting in the garage unused. A good bike is an investment that can provide you with healthy enjoyment for years. It could even save you money on health care costs by being healthier, and it's a great way to meet new people.

Numerous studies show that people who bike regularly are leaner, fitter, have better triglyceride levels, lower blood pressure, better insulin levels, higher self-esteem and better mental health. Who doesn't want all that? In 2007, *Cycling & Health* published a study that said the benefits of biking outweighed the risks by 20 to 1.

Recommendation: Go to a real bike shop (they're the places that repair bikes, not just sell them) on a fact-finding mission. Talk, ask, learn and take a free test ride. I guarantee you'll be glad you did.

Biking health benefits and how to get started videos:

http://www.bestplacestoliveretire.com/2015/02/bi king-healthy-retirement-activity.html

Under the Stars

There's just something special about sitting around a roaring fire out in the wilderness (even if it's only a few miles from your home and it's located in the suburbs) and looking up at a sky full of stars while breathing in fresh clean out door air. It's almost spiritual. There are also special laws that apply to camping that you may not be aware of. Any food you make while camping will taste far better than the same food made at home. Everything from simple conversation to sipping your favorite beverage is more enjoyable when it's done sitting in the glow of a campsite fire.

Thanks to improved technology, today's camping equipment is inexpensive and comfortable. You can get a 4-6 man tent (for extra space), a queen-size bed that inflates on its own, and a couple of warm sleeping bags and a few other items like lighting for a few hundred bucks.

I'm not much for roughing it for long periods of time. When I tent camp, I do it one night at a time. I go out, set up, build a fire, enjoy some great food, drink and company and head home the next morning. Unless a long hike or bike is also planned, which it usually is. Of course, some people prefer to do their camping in an RV. Either way, getting out into nature overnight reduces stress and does something for the soul unmatched by most other activities.

If you haven't gone camping in a long time or have

never been, you really should consider it as a pursuit during your retirement years. Combined with hiking, biking or other activities you enjoy, it can add excitement and richness to your life while also improving your health.

Take a trip to a sports or outdoor specialty shop to look around and learn—it's free. Go online and see what private campgrounds, state and national parks offer camping nearby. Spend a few nights under the stars, and who knows, maybe you'll plan a long-distance camping trip across the country. You may save a lot of money over staying in hotels and have far more fun. Boondocking or rouge camping is free and can be a snowbird option for those on a strict retirement budget. For camping videos and resources go to:

http://www.bestplacestoliveretire.com/2015/02/camping-ideal-retirement-pursuit.html

Enjoyable at Any Age

This is one pursuit that will get you off the couch and outdoors among beautiful scenery and breathing fresh outdoor air for hours of fun. If you use a golf pull cart, a lightweight cart that allows you to pull or push your golf bag and clubs around the course with little effort, and walk the course, you'll get far more than your new job's required one hour of daily exercise even if you play only nine holes. Visit any course in Florida with lower rates during the winter months if you need proof that you can play this game at any age.

You can start playing with just a small investment in equipment. You could start playing without taking lessons, but learning the right way to hold a club, stand, swing, etc., makes playing a round of golf much more fun, especially because you can laugh at how the people who never took lessons play. What if you still can't play golf well, even after lessons? That's why they make alcohol. The worse you play, the more you're supposed to drink. You'll have more fun and be more amusing to others.

Golf Improvement Clubs

Almost everyone will experience instant "game improvement" with a good set of clubs because of better technology. Yes, they'll cost a little more, but you'll play better and have more fun with better clubs. If cheap or garage sale clubs are all you can afford, don't let that stop you. You can still have a blast in the beautiful outdoors, but it may involve more alcohol.

Tips

- Buy "oversize" clubs. The club face is slightly larger, so they are a lot more forgiving. You're out there to have fun.
- Golf is a lot more fun playing with company. Try to get a few friends or relatives addicted to the game and play on regular schedule. Many doctors play every Wednesday, for instance.
- If cash is tight, check the websites of different courses for special reduced rates, like "twilight" rates. Golfing after 2:00 p.m. and on weekdays when the working schmucks can't play usually means significant savings. Retirement has its

benefits. Make sure to have plenty of cold refreshment if playing in hot weather.

For golf videos and resources go to:

http://www.bestplacestoliveretire.com/2015/02/go lf-is-ideal-active-outdoor-activity.html

Ride Up Have Fun Getting Down

Please hear me out on this one. There is a reason that millions of people all around the world actually look forward to snow. The ski link below will take you to a page where you can see a 95½ year-old man skiing and loving it. That's right: While some people dread even the thought of it, lots of people of all ages, including seniors in their 70's and 80's and beyond, dream of fresh snow. The joy of a day on the slopes followed by beverages by the roaring fire in the lodge or at a favorite slope-side apres-ski (after ski) pub can't be beat.

Can't stand cold weather? Ski shops carry outerwear you won't find at regular stores that just sell "fashion" jackets and coats. Did you ever see those guys on an expedition at the North Pole on TV? Outdoor specialty stores like ski shops have fashionable clothing that will keep you warm and comfortable regardless of the temperature on the slopes. Imagine the additional possibilities for fun, excitement, exercise and social opportunities you could enjoy if you discovered that you actually love to ski.

Almost every ski area now offers special learn-to-ski packages. The package includes being properly fitted for rental ski equipment for the day, a pass to the easier gentler slopes, and most importantly, a ski lesson. If you've never skied before, you just may have the time of your life and gain a reason to look forward to all four seasons.

Ski areas take the safety of their guests very seriously today. While not required, many skiers now wear helmets, just like most daily bike riders do. After just one lesson, you will know the basics and can ski at your own pace. Skiing is about more than just the thrill of going down a mountain on your own power. It's about the spectacular winter scenery that only those that venture up the ski lifts to the top of the mountain (but not when you're learning) are privy to. It's about meeting new people sitting next to you on the lifts and sharing conversation on the way up the mountain. It's about the rustic charm, friendliness and warmth of the resorts and surrounding businesses that cater to skiers usually exude.

In the name of excitement and adventure, you owe it to yourself to spend one day to see if skiing is something that will add richness to your life. Skiing is similar to biking in that you can enjoy the outdoors while getting exercise and expand your social circle too if you wish.

If you haven't skied for decades, you'll discover that like cars today, ski equipment technology has advanced so you learn to turn and stay in control much easier and quicker today. The cost of skiing, once you invest in good equipment that will last for years, can be very reasonable. Most ski areas offer bargain season passes that allow you to ski anytime Monday through Friday. You'll save money, and you won't have to put up with the weekend crowds and long lift lines. Most also offer steep discounts and even free skiing to seniors.

Ski clubs are available to join just about everywhere there are slopes. Joining a Ski club offers you the ability to meet all requirements of your new job of retirement by joining a community of people, getting exercise and having fun. Then you'll join the happier, healthier millions of people around the world that actually look forward to winter and snow.

For videos and resources on skiing go to:

http://www.bestplacestoliveretire.com/2014/11/ski ing-how-live-longer-healthier-happier-life.html

No Mountains Required

This is how to enjoy nature while getting a great workout during the winter and mountains; lift tickets or season passes aren't necessary. The equipment is different from downhill skiing, and getting equipped at a local Nordic ski equipment shop is essential because they will know what you'll need to enjoy the trails in your particular area.

There are many advantages to this type of winter fun. The equipment can cost less than downhill skiing equipment. Once you're equipped, there are usually many free trails you can use to enjoy the beautiful scenery, peace and quiet of winter wilderness.

State, national and even many city parks are great places to enjoy this type of skiing without having to pay any kind of fee. There's no better exercise either, because it's no impact, and you're using both your arms and legs. It's a sport you can become good at the first day. Learning from someone experienced isn't as necessary as downhill skiing, but it's not a bad idea.

Cross-country skiing is what adventurous, fun-loving, healthy people do when there's snow on the ground instead of running or biking. There are clubs of wonderful people to enjoy this sport with too, so you can meet all the requirements of your new job all winter long. Many clubs schedule daily skiing that includes stopping at restaurants or pubs. If you'll be retiring where there's a winter to enjoy, this is an activity that can greatly enhance your life even if you're on a strict budget. For videos and more go to:

http://www.bestplacestoliveretire.com/2015/02/cross-country-skiing-is-excellent-pursuit.html

The Worst Day Doing This Is Better Than

Fishing is a wonderful way to get exercise while doing something that melts away stress. It's a pursuit that can be enjoyed for a lifetime. Getting out into nature and soaking up some beautiful water views is good for the mind and soul, and it's an activity that both men and women can enjoy.

The cost of getting started is very affordable, and the one-time investment in good equipment can provide years of enjoyment. Like skiing, there's more to fishing than just trying to land a fish. It's the adventure of trying out a new place to fish. It's the excitement every time you get a nibble that might yield a trophy-size fish. It's walking out in nature and breathing the fresh air while getting to and from that special fishing hole or walking along the beach. It's about taking home the day's best catch and having an excellent healthy dinner with fish you know is fresh.

Many states offer retirees special low rates on fishing licenses. Like most of these sports, you could spend a lot of money if you wanted to by buying a boat or hiring professional fishing guides to take you to the most productive places, but you can have just as much fun without spending a buck.

Depending upon where you will be living or traveling while retired, you may also enjoy clamming, crabbing or hunting for oysters or lobster. A one-time investment of a couple hundred bucks into a kayak could add yet another adventurous aspect to your fishing trips by getting you out onto the water. Fishing could be the perfect activity to make living in an area near rivers, lakes or beaches more adventurous.

http://www.bestplacestoliveretire.com/2015/02/fishing-is-great-outdoor-fun.html

Done at Any Age with Multiple Benefits

Gardening is a form of no-impact moderate outdoor exercise that also relaxes and reduces stress. You can get your entire recommended daily requirement of physical activity tending to your garden while growing your own fruits and vegetables. You can save money on food while enjoying better tasting, healthier produce. Studies show that there's more to produce than just vitamins and minerals. There are more micro-nutrients that improve health and prevent disease being found in fruits and vegetables almost every day by research scientists. However, after produce has been harvested, it slowly starts to lose its magical health benefits, so the healthiest vegetables are the ones harvested as close to eating as possible, like the produce from your garden that goes right onto your table. Growing your own food without using pesticides and chemicals will allow you to enjoy organic produce for less than it would cost at the grocery store.

If you have the space, gardening is an ideal pursuit to add health and variety to your after-work life. It costs next to nothing for a few simple hand tools, seeds and fencing. Gardening is a pursuit that can be enjoyed at any age while you get your exercise. Gardening clubs are an excellent way to join a community and further increase your enjoyment. Even a small plot can yield enough for tasty, healthy salads. If you have the space, gardening along with other pursuits can be part of a healthy and rewarding retirement.

http://www.bestplacestoliveretire.com/2015/02/gardening-is-healthy-exercise.html

Ancient Gifts from Afar

Yoga is known to increase flexibility, muscle strength, muscle tone, respiration, and energy. That's why it's one of the fastest growing activities for men and women of all ages. It can help with weight loss and balance our metabolism. It can also improve our ability to perform other physical activities and help protect us from injury. While yoga is long known for lowering stress levels, blood pressure and heart rate, studies have also shown that yoga can reduce triglyceride and cholesterol levels. Do you how many toxic prescription drugs you'd have to consume to accomplish all of that?

The great thing about yoga is that just about anyone at any age can do it, and the cost of yoga gear isn't expensive. The cost of classes at yoga studios can vary, but many offer free or low-cost beginner classes. While most yoga instructors agree that taking classes in the beginning may be the best way to go, there are videos and classes available online for free. If you're a man and worried about the no doubt endless jokes that would result from the guys if they saw you walking into a yoga studio, or you're worried about others checking out your rear view as you pose, you can find free online classes by following the yoga link below.

Afraid of getting involved in yoga because you think it will eventually lead to you being required to wear tight, almost-see through yoga pants? Then you may want to consider Tai Chi. It's a martial art that relieves stress and has all the same health benefits as yoga, but you get to wear cool, loose-fitting karate type robes instead of tights. Both yoga and Tai Chi can involve classes where you become connected to a community while getting your required healthy exercise. Again, if you try it, you may find something that will make you healthier that you will enjoy for the rest of your life. For videos and more go to:

http://www.bestplacestoliveretire.com/2015/02/yoga-martial-arts-healthyt-any-age.html

Learn to Do This the Best You Can

There was a time in America when families looked forward to dinner and sat down to a meal mainly cooked from scratch. In countries where people live the longest, healthiest lives, they still do just that. To them, every meal is always something special. It's not just about the food; it's about taking the time to relax while connecting and enjoying good company and conversation.

Now that you're retired, you too can make a decision that meals at home will be far more enjoyable than eating out, especially if that involves huge neon signs, a dollar menu or drive-thru. What's that? Every time you cook, smoke fills the house? Then take cooking classes at a local college or buy a cookbook and teach yourself.

For instance, if you love spaghetti and lasagna, buy an Italian cookbook and once or twice a week, pick out a recipe that looks good. Make a list and head to the grocery store and get the required ingredients. Do some quick research and get a bottle of wine that will go with the meal you're preparing. It's actually fun to make a big deal of getting the freshest ingredients and taking the necessary time to prepare a great meal.

Get an extra bottle of wine to sip while cooking (not recommended for beginners). Get your significant other if you have one, involved in the whole process. Or invite some new friends from the bike club you just joined. Use your best china and crystal. If meals at home have become nothing but opening a can of *this* or throwing *that* in the microwave, you'll be amazed how rewarding this can be. Get a new cookbook every month, and in about a year, the meals you enjoy at home could be tastier, healthier and more enjoyable than any restaurant in town serves.

Shopping for the perfect ingredients, preparing and

serving a great meal may involve enough physical activity for you to meet your daily one-hour requirement. Sharing your meal with others can help you meet the community requirement. Why not arrange a spaghetti night with family or friends every week? And yes, there are cooking and dinner clubs where people get together to enjoy each other's company and cooking. We all have to eat, so why not make something special of it?

http://www.bestplacestoliveretire.com/2015/02/learning-to-cook-has-benefits.html

Capturing Beauty and Great Times

Photography is a pursuit that anyone can become quite good at it today, thanks once again to improved technology. Photography can be the perfect companion pursuit to walking, hiking or just about any other outdoor activity we've covered so far. Why not take a close-up pic of that gorgeous rose you grew in your garden, that magnificent winter scene from from the ski lift, or a picture of every shared spaghetti night?

An inexpensive small digital camera that can fit in your pocket can open up a whole new world. Who knows what that seed might grow into? Maybe your own framed art decorating your living room? Perhaps selling copies online to bloggers looking for unique pictures to add to their posts.

Maybe you'll become the designated picture taker on rides your bike club takes. You may enjoy it so much you'll plan walks, hikes, or cross country ski trips to take pictures of specific places. And yes, you can join a photography club or start your own. Wow, your "retirement" is starting to sound pretty great!

http://www.bestplacestoliveretire.com/2015/02/lea rn-photograpy-fun-income.html

I Always Wanted to Learn to [insert your desire]!

Always wanted to learn how to paint? Wish you knew more about woodworking so you could make furniture? If you're retired, now is the time to do something about it. Really, why put it off any longer? How do you know you aren't a great craftsman, painter or musician unless you try? Too old? Have you seen how many wrinkled, balding gray-haired rock stars there are delighting 18-year-old's? If it's something you've always wanted to do, just do it!

Many colleges have classes specifically for seniors. Many retirees have gone back to school to learn a new career or just for the fun of it. Many colleges offer free or reduced tuition for retirees. These days, you're never too old to go back to school. Remember, if you meet the exercise requirement of your new job of retirement, you may have a very long, healthy life in front of you.

It's all about taking that first step and enrolling for that college course or signing up for the community center's art class. Enjoying your life is one of your new job requirements. If learning is something you want to do, take that first step.

Live In a Town Like This

Many people who live the longest, healthiest and

happiest lives have this in common: They live in towns that have shops, restaurants and pubs and almost everything they need within walking distance. So they walk a lot, every day. Many don't even own a car.

What if golfing, skiing, biking or all of the previously covered pursuits don't sound good to you? No problem. If you move to a very walkable town where produce markets, grocery stores, doctors and pharmacies are all within walking distance, you'll stay healthy by getting your "exercise" just going about your daily life. You'll get to know your neighbors and others people in town because they'll be out walking every day too. You can get your required exercise and become part of a new pack just by living in the right location.

The median cost of car ownership in the US at the time of this book's writing was over $9100 a year, according to *Consumer Reports*. Yes, the accumulated cost of gas, insurance, oil changes, tires, depreciation, registration and other auto expenses consumes a lot of your retirement cash. Living in a safe town where all your needs can met by walking or biking can not only provide you with the life extending exercise, it can put about $758 more dollars in your retirement pocket every month.

The Bottom Line

There's a very real possibility that you may love to walk, hike, bike and ski. These pursuits may bring you a happier, more adventurous retirement than you ever imagined. It would be a shame if you missed out the joy they could bring and settle for a retirement of

163

boredom because you never tried even tried them, wouldn't it?

For Videos and Retirement Pursuit Resources:

http://www.bestplacestoliveretire.com/2015/02/how-to-live-longer-healthier-life.html

Summary and Tips

- Start asking yourself "If time and money were no object and I could be doing anything I wanted at this very moment, what would it be? If I could be anywhere I wanted to be right now, where would I be?"

- Make a list of all the things you like to do in life before you cash in your chips. Pick the one that turns you on the most and start making plans now to do it.

- Make a list of all the places you would like to see before you die. Pick the one that you most would like to visit and start making plans to go. What? You say you can't because [insert excuse that stands between you and your dream]? Forget that and start asking yourself "How can I make this happen?"

- Having a hard time coming up with anything you really desire to do? Head to a large sporting goods store, RV dealer, or travel show and start looking and learning. Don't jump in with a large purchase; just take some time for yourself for once. See what's out there. Take that bike or RV—or both—for a test ride. Try the "learn to" ski or golf package. You just might love it.

- Try adding at least one pursuit to your life that

satisfies all three responsibilities of your new job, getting one hour of exercise, becoming part of a new group of people, and having fun!

Generating Cash and Write-Offs in Retirement

The last thing you may want to do in retirement is to create a job for yourself that requires you to do something you don't want to do and robs you of your free time. That's not what this chapter is about. This chapter is about generating money doing something you enjoy and on your own schedule. It's also about increasing the amount of cash you have to spend because of legally being allowed to write-off your car, home and travel because it's part of your business. For instance, you could tie making money into a RV snowbird lifestyle and write off your winters' travel in warm destinations.

Starting a small business for between $100-$1000 that you can almost entirely work when, where and if you want, may be an ideal addition to your retirement plan, especially if it's something you love to do and it's tied into your other plans for retirement. We'll cover a few different ways to earn cash and gain write offs.

Humidors Cookies Bird-feeders

There has probably never been a better time in the last 50 years than now to sell handcrafted or specially made goods in the US. Many people today are tired of mass produced, poorly made machine manufactured products from less than friendly foreign countries. Many consumers today are looking for higher quality, unique, handcrafted or special goods and are often willing to pay considerably more for quality products or products with a story behind them. This is especially true for handcrafted products made in the USA, guaranteed to be free of toxic materials.

New farmers' markets are opening that allow only vendors that sell products they've made themselves; no mass produced t-shirts or handbags are allowed. There are many sites like Etsy.com that allow only handcrafted goods or special vintage items to be offered for sale. One visit to Etsy will prove to you that there is a market for just about any kind of handmade product you can think of. You can check the prices, reviews and other stats of the best-selling vendors now selling what you'd like to gather information.

Making and selling your own unique items has several advantages over just buying manufactured products from a wholesaler and offering them for sale. Vendors who buy a mass-produced product from a wholesaler or distributor have to compete with all the other people who are selling the same thing. You see this on Ebay all the time, where dozens of sellers of the same products lower their price to get an edge, but then so does everybody else. This race to the bottom piece war ends when everyone is priced so low no one can make a profit. That won't happen with your unique one-of-a-kind birdhouses, each one numbered and signed by you.

When you are selling "Birdhouses Handcrafted by [insert your name] of [insert your town, state]" you have no competition. No competitor can buy the same thing from a wholesaler and undercut your price because your product is unique, handcrafted and special. Maybe you sign and number each birdhouse or framed bird photograph you create. Maybe your thing is that you never make the same exact birdhouse twice, or never sell more than one framed, signed copy of that wildlife photograph. The proud purchaser of your product can boast to his friends, "yea, it was handcrafted by [your name] and he'll never make another one like it, so I have the only one.

As an "artist" who creates products, you have many different ways to sell your goods to eager buyers. You could choose just one or use many of them. You could choose to sell only online through your own website or on sites like Etsy. You could sell at local flea markets and farmers' markets. Farmers markets that allow vendors to sell only goods they've made themselves can be very lucrative because customers who flock to these outlets are usually more affluent and are willing to pay more for something that is unique and special. Maybe your birdhouses are painted the colors of the birds that the house was built to be a home for.

There are many art festivals, craft fairs and other

events that are held throughout the US, especially in the warm winter locations when millions of affluent snowbirds flock there. Many allow only vendors selling quality handmade goods. You may be able to sell a lot of your merchandise in a very short period of time at relatively high prices at such events.

Interested in making something special you're interested in, but don't have the skills? Why not take a course at a community college?

RV Lifestyle Meets Money Making Business

Maybe you'll decide to retire in place to stay connected to your family and longtime friends and snowbird in an RV every winter. Why not fill an enclosed trailer with your special birdhouses, large framed wildlife art or homemade cookies sealed in attractive tins and hit the festival circuit every winter when things heat up in snowbird locations.

Many annual festivals are held during the winter when millions of affluent snowbirds head south and are looking for places to go. You could sell a lot of your goods at very high prices during these events. The best thing is, if you do it right, you may be able to write off some of your RV winter snowbirding because you're there to do business. What could be better than meeting new people from all over the world while you're making money in the sunshine and fresh air in a beautiful palm tree setting?

Other $100-$1000 Start Up Ideas

Do you have some specialized knowledge that may be able to help others? If you have a way to help people, you may be able to earn income working when and if you want, and to afford better to enjoy your retirement through consulting or becoming a coach. You may not need anything more than your cell phone, a $10-a-month website, and a Paypal account to accept payment to get started. This type of income generation is great because you can work from home while snowbirding in Florida or even living overseas.

Rather than becoming a "career" coach like thousands of others, advertise yourself as a nursing career coach, a restaurant cook career coach, or be a mom coach, for instance. There are people out there right now who desperately need advice, but don't have anyone to go to or don't want to ask the people they now know for fear of embarrassment or other personal reasons. Maybe they have questions about parenting that they can't find answers online to and don't want to ask their parents because they don't think they did such a good job.

You probably have experience in something that could really help someone. There are people out there who need advice or answers about something you have years of experience at. You may be able to help them out and earn $100 or more an hour. This is a business service where charging too little can actually hurt you because you won't be considered an expert. Charge a rate of at least $100 per hour. You may want to search for and join a related association online for credential purposes.

You can offer a 20-minute session for only $39 and offer many other price points and plans. You probably won't get 40 hours of "work" a week, but you're retired, so you don't want that anyway. If you got only four hours of work a month, could you find a way to spend an extra $400+? You can feel good about yourself because you're helping someone out and earning extra money just for talking on the phone. Best of all, you can do this from home or in Florida during the winter or while living overseas.

Easy Sell Something Start-Ups

There's no easier way to make extra cash than selling something for more than you paid for it. Is there a hobby that you enjoy that you can make money with by sharing it with others? Love trains and train sets? Why not buy them at garage sales and on craigslist and resell them on Ebay, Amazon, or your own website? You can also sell them at special shows or flea markets while you travel the US in your RV during the winter.

Going to snowbird or travel in warmer parts of the US during winter? Why not buy everything you find that has to do with retirement while shopping garage sales while you're home? Then you might sell them at flea markets in snowbird areas during the winter when you're down there. Do you think any of the retirees that flock to these events would buy a "Goodbye Tension, Hello Pension" coffee mug or t-shirt from you? You bet they would!

What are you interested in? Nothing? You just like to drink? Specialize in selling beer steins, beer mugs and shot glasses. Buy them at garage sales and thrift stores and list them on Ebay while at home. Sell them at the packed flea markets while in snowbird destinations during the winter.

Consider Modeling

No, I'm not suggesting that you try to earn money by modeling bathing suits. What I'm referring to is the practice of finding someone who is successful doing something that you'd like to do, then becoming successful yourself doing the same thing.

It works like this. You see someone selling lots of expensive handmade [insert something you're interested in] on Etsy. The concept of modeling holds that if you do the same things that a successful business does, you too are likely to be successful. The opposite of modeling would be to just come up with an idea and use trial and error to make the business work. Modeling a business that is already working will mean you are less likely to try something that's already been proven not to work.

To "model" a business, you would learn what makes them successful. What makes their products more desirable than the competitions? How do they price? Do they offer their customers a better guarantee than the others do? Do they describe their products better or include actual dimensions where the other sellers don't bother? You may even order one of their products to see how it's shipped and packaged and compare the quality of their offering against what you will offer.

You won't be copying their product, but knowing if your product is of higher, lower or roughly the same quality can help. What you will be doing is learning the practices that help make them successful and improving on the ones you think are weak.

If you do as well or better than your competitor in

173

marketing products, and your goods are of similar or higher quality, you have a good chance of being successful. If your product offers more quality that theirs, you can price with confidence at around the same amount or a little higher. If your product doesn't quite measure up, you know you need to price lower or improve your offering.

For videos and resources on starting a business in retirement go to:

http://www.bestplacestoliveretire.com/2015/02/how-start-your-own-small-business.html

Retirement Destroyers

I write this chapter risking the possibility that someone will read this book and write a review somewhere saying "'It was too negative," but knowing what has caused retirement disasters and regret for others may help prevent that from happening to you.

Fear and Indecision

You're daydreaming about doing something wonderful when you retire. Maybe you're feeling a sense of adventure, excitement and freedom as you daydream about driving an RV and rolling down the road towards Yellowstone National Park. You have the window rolled down because it's sunny and warm and the air smells fresh and clean. You aren't worried about your old work place because you're never going back. You aren't worried about the kids burning down the house while you're away because they have their own homes now. You're completely relaxed and enjoying and enjoying this amazing feeling. It's a different feeling because for the first time in decades you feel truly free and secure. You have no deadlines or schedules to meet. You have a secure, fixed income and no real money concerns. Everything's perfect in this daydream.

Suddenly that wonderful feeling is invaded by negative thoughts. Can you afford an RV? What if you get into an accident? Or get lost and end up in a bad area somewhere?

We are naturally fearful of the unknown. Many of our fears are unfounded or vague. Other fears are the result of sensational stories of doom being magnified by news sources for the sole purpose of selling newspapers and subscriptions to earn a profit. Maybe your daydream was interrupted by an unease that you can't define and have no idea where it's coming from.

Hey, you sacrificed your whole life, did the right thing and took care of all your responsibilities for decades. Now it's your turn to do what you really want. One study showed that 95% of what we worry about never happens, yet we waste precious time and energy worrying about things that will never happen. Don't let unfounded fears or vague nagging doubts rob you of the exciting, adventurous retirement you deserve.

If fear or doubt is holding you back from looking into something you want to do, are those fears real or not? For example, let's say you really want to [insert dream], but doubts are causing indecision, so you do nothing. What to do?

Get out a piece of paper and write "what are the

worst possible things that could happen if I go ahead and [insert dream]?" List any and all doubts or fears. Don't wonder if you should write a thought down or not—just write down everything without holding back. Do this daily until you can't possibly come up with any more concerns to write down. Then go down the list and cross off the fears or doubts that are sheer nonsense. After doing that, of the reasons that are left (if any), does it make sense to give up on [insert dream] for those reasons?

Maybe one fear left on the paper is a concern about not being able to afford an RV. That's a valid concern, but it's probably there simply because you don't have enough information. It's probably there because you don't know what type of RV would best meet your needs or how much they cost.

Solution? Free online research and exploratory trips to RV dealers will give you the information you need to know if you can afford it or not. A good salesman may able to show you models that will meet your needs and how you can afford them. RV's can be financed over a long period of time, making the payments smaller. You may be able to deduct the interest as a "second home" if it qualifies, making it even more affordable. After gathering all of the information, you'll know if you can afford it or not, but don't allow unfounded fears rob you of your dreams, because they may indeed be possible to achieve.

Important Relationship Neglect

Most people would think that divorce must be extremely rare among retirees. Yet between 1990 and

2010, the number of divorces involving spouses over 50 years old went up by 100%. In 2010, people 50 or older accounted for 25% of all divorces in the US.

In retirement, two people can live almost as cheaply as one. Divorce in retirement often results in a much lower standard of living for both affected parties. While divorce proceedings between long term spouses can start out friendly, they often turn ugly, resulting in high legal fees that can cook nest eggs. It's tough enough to recover from divorce while still working. It's nearly impossible during retirement on a fixed income.

Both married couples and those living unmarried with a long-time significant other should individually do the questionnaires in this book, about what they want their retirement to look like. During the routine of a working life, a couple could get along well for decades because of the needs of the kids or their employers without ever knowing specifically what the other wants retirement to look like.

Couples that talk about retirement often, but in vague terms while still working, may never know that they have entirely different ideas of what an ideal retirement will look like until the day arrives. What if one partner has always pictured retirement as making things out of wood in the garage and being a homebody, and the other partner sees retirement as a time to travel the world?

Couples should do the questionnaires in a later chapter and share them with each other. This way you'll see where your retirement visions are similar and where they don't match up. If one of the strongest desires for both of you is traveling overseas, great. If the strongest desire for one is travel and the strongest for the other is woodworking at home, it's time to work together to find a compromise. Traveling together part of each year and staying home the rest of the year, with one partner working with wood in the garage while the other is busy planning next year's trip, may be an ideal solution.

Too Cold to Too Hot

As a real estate broker in Florida for nearly two decades, I sold lots of homes to people who were moving to the sunshine state for the warm weather. I later sold many homes for those same people, who were moving out of Florida because it was too hot for them.

Florida's a lot closer to the equator than the state those people moved from, so summer-like weather often started in March or April. That weather often lasted until October or November. Many were not counting on uncomfortable summer-like weather lasting up to nine months a year or the high electric bills from the constant running of the AC during all those months. Most years, the only time it's "warm" (not hot) in Florida is three months during the winter. Other popular "warm weather" states like Arizona and Nevada also have more hot weather than newcomers anticipate. Millions of people have relocated "permanently" to a warm location, only to move back.

As I'm writing this paragraph in early 2015, climate scientists just announced that the hottest year on record globally was 2014. Globally, nine of the ten

179

hottest Junes on record happened since the year 2000.

Much has changed since the days when many of our grandparents moved south for retirement. The weather is getting warmer, and we are expected to live much longer. With winters in the north getting milder and land and water temperature heating up in the southern states, should you really be moving south for a retirement that could last many decades?

Many people in the US don't buy into the science of global warming or don't think it will affect them personally. Taking a trip to Glacier National Park in Montana may provide insight that they can see with their own eyes. When the park was first established in 1910, there were over 150 Glaciers there, hence the name. Traveling to the park today, visitors will only be able to see what's left of 25 of them, because the others have melted and are gone. If you want to visit the park because you've never seen a glacier before, be sure to do so before 2020 because climate scientists say they may all be gone by 2020. Winters in Montana just aren't as cold as they once were.

To preserve your retirement and any money you've managed to save, you'll probably want to plan where you live during retirement carefully. Spending a lot of money moving somewhere that's a mistake can consume a lot of your precious time and money. The expense of multiple long distance moves combined with the expenses of multiple home purchases and selling can threaten a retirement.

Trouble Shedding Your Old Work Identity

I once had a business associate who had spent decades building a large, successful business. The business made him very wealthy. He devoted so much time and effort to building it, his personal and family life suffered. He was divorced young and often complained that no matter how much money he gave his kids, his relationship with them was never good.

When he turned 65, he sold his business to finally live the life he worked all of his life for. He said he'd been planning for it financially forever and was hoping that he could use the free time to finally relax and develop good relationships with his now older adult children

He sold his business for millions. He died of cancer just seven months later. Some guessed that the cancer manifested itself because he was sick the about the changes the new owners made to "his" business. His short retirement was spent obsessing over the business he cashed out of, but couldn't mentally separate himself from.

It's not hard to understand how it can be hard to let go of your work life. Waking up and getting ready to go to work is a habit that we've developed over decades. It became a part of our life, the same as eating, drinking or sleeping. Having a habit that's been burned into memory and repeated 1000's of times is hard to change.

That's why it's crucial to have a retirement plan, so you can start developing new habits for your brain to run instead of it trying to run the old work routine every Monday to Friday. Having exciting adventurous pursuits you can start doing right after retirement, especially if they involve physical activity, new packs of people to replace the old ones from work, and fun, will help you shed your old life and get on with enjoying your new one.

No Plan Can be Hazardous to Your Retirement

Research published in the Journal of the American Heart Association showed that watching TV for three hours or more each day can increase the risk of premature death from any cause by 200%. I'm sure you didn't sacrifice your whole life just to experience a retirement of boredom, mild depression associated with TV viewing and increased chance of premature death.

Entering retirement without a plan of how you are going to enjoy it, is like sailing out into the ocean in a boat without a rudder. The wind will decide where you'll go, and you may end up shipwrecked on the rocks. Being faced with long days and nothing specific planned could lead to just sitting motionless on the couch watching TV for hours. That could quickly become a habit that is difficult to change. Having no plan, or a vague plan to "just relax," could lead to years of boredom and declining health. Doesn't a plan of meeting new people, getting physical exercise in a manner you enjoy and getting healthy sound like a good alternative?

Having said that, you deserve to do anything you wish during the retirement you earned, including watching TV all day if that makes you happy.

Living Longer and Healthier

Just like your car, the better you take care of yourself, the better it will operate and the longer it will last. Unfortunately, unlike a car, you didn't come with a warranty, and when it doesn't work right, you can't trade it in for a new one. Statistically, you're likely to live for a very long time past the normal retirement age. Emerging research shows that pain and suffering need not be a part of aging. In fact, if we put forth the effort to stay active in retirement, we can enjoy most of that time feeling even better than when we were working and may not have had the time to take care of ourselves, as we have in retirement.

Alternative for People Who Hate Exercise

You can live a long, healthy life without ever buying a piece of exercise equipment or stepping one foot in a gym. If you have exercise equipment at home or belong to a gym that's fantastic, but how do people who always hated sports and exercise live a healthy long life?

National Geographic sponsored a study on areas of the world where people lived the longest healthiest lives. These people didn't exercise as we Americans know it, but daily physical activity was just a part of their normal everyday life. The people studied mostly lived in small towns. When they went to restaurants, shops or to visit with friends and family, they walked. One faith-based group they studied here in the US went on community hikes regularly.

If you're planning to sell your home to cash in on the tax-free profit and relocate or right-size, why not move to a very walkable town? This could be a friendly small town or a large city where just about everywhere you need to go each day, you can get to by walking or biking. There are exciting places to live, like the college or outdoor towns covered in this book, or found through links provided, where you can do just that.

What Is This Really Costing You

There are towns you can live in where you really don't need a car. You could save the estimated $750 a month a car costs, when depreciation and the total cost of ownership is included, according to *Consumer Reports*. If you choose to travel and live overseas, a lifestyle covered in this book, you won't need a car. You can use your savings towards airline tickets and taxis.

You May Want to Know This

How much activity are you getting during your normal daily routine? If you're not sure, you may want to make a small investment in a pedometer. They're small devices that look like a watch and will count how many steps you're taking in a day. One common suggested goal is 10,000 steps or the equivalent of a five-mile walk. They can be bought for as little as $25.

From the Dirt

Gardening was a common main activity done by two of the three groups of people who may live the longest, healthiest lives on earth and featured in The Blue Zone studies. Even more compelling were factors that all three of these groups of people had in common: They put family first, had strong ties to their community or faith, were socially active, didn't smoke, consumed beans as a regular part of their diet, and physical activity was an inseparable part of their daily life.

US Guidelines for Longer, Healthier Lives

The U.S. Department of Health and Human Service's physical activity guidelines recommend a minimum of 2.5 hours a week of moderate aerobic activity, like walking. An hour and 15 minutes a week of vigorous aerobic activity such as jogging would also meet the minimum requirements. US government health authorities also recommend muscle-strengthening activities that involve all major muscle groups at least two days a week.

The above guidelines are the *minimum* physical activity recommended to reduce the risk of chronic diseases and increase our chances of living longer. Unfortunately, only 20% of us are meeting this minimum, as reported by the Centers for Disease Control and Prevention in May 2013.

My research shows that to lower our risk of disease substantially and give ourselves the best chance of living a long active healthy life, an hour a day of moderate aerobic activity daily is needed. Two of those days every week should include strength training, such as weights.

I know I may seem overly optimistic about getting us to exercise more than the minimum, when only 20% are doing the least amount possible; however, since you've made the effort of buying and reading a book titled *How to Retire Happier*, I believe you may have the motivation and desire to do what it takes to live longer, healthier and happier.

People who don't particularly care about living longer and healthier don't need to worry about exercising. Those who are only minimally concerned can do the minimum as recommended by US guidelines. People like you who want the most out of your life will find a way to get exercise an hour every day—and enjoy it. It works because that's how our bodies were designed to function.

Good or Bad Health Domino Effect

Discovering just one daily physical activity you love will likely lead to developing other positive habits. Exercise is considered a "keystone habit." A keystone habit is a one that often leads to developing other similar habits. Developing a healthy keystone habit can lead to many more positive habits. Unfortunately, the opposite is also true.

For instance, if a new retiree develops a habit of TV viewing for much of the day, that may lead to a daily habit of snacking on unhealthy junk food while sitting on the couch. That's why it's so important to develop a plan of how you're going to make your retirement exciting and healthful if you're interested in living a long, adventurous and healthy life.

It Only Takes Effort at First

What if you're really out of shape and overweight? See your doctor and tell him you are going to start [insert activity that could save your life] and you want to make sure you're in good enough health to get started. When your doctor gives you the OK, start slow and just try to do a little more each day. If it takes you six months to work up to an hour's worth of walking a day, that's better than overdoing it the first day and quitting the next because you're in excruciating pain.

What if you aren't really interested in doing any physical activity? See if you can convince yourself to visit a real bike shop and take a test drive, or find some other activity that you can do for about two months. According to latest findings on habit formation, you have to make an effort to stick with it for only about 62 days. By that time it should become a habit, and you'll likely do it automatically.

Doing the activity at the same time every day, like right after breakfast or lunch, will help the habit form if you're having a hard time. After about 62 days, your brain will cue up that habit without you even having to think about it. It'll be like your brain telling your body it's time to [insert activity] because it's after lunch, just as you breathe automatically without having to think about it.

Getting Healthier as You Age Is Possible

There has never been a better time to be your age. There are far more ways for retirees to enjoy life now than were available to our parents and grandparents.

There are ski, bike, garden and all kinds of clubs that you have to be 55 or older just to join. There's golf communities you can't buy a home or condo in unless you're old enough. Ski areas offer special discounts, cheaper season passes, and even free skiing for those of us who have attained a certain age.

Staying connected and socially active is one of the secrets to living a longer healthier life. Luckily, most of us can stop working when we're still quite healthy and capable of physical activity. Because of medical advances, even if we have a bad knee or shoulder, we can get it replaced and get on with our life.

We have been given more choices and opportunities today for fun and adventure than any previous generation. What would you rather be doing one evening 30 days from now, sitting on the couch watching a rerun you've seen for the sixth time or sitting around the fire with a drink laughing with your RV buddies after hiking all afternoon and enjoying a great outdoor dinner made on the grill?

There are RV groups of like-minded people who travel the county together or return to the same RV community every year to snowbird and enjoy life. That wouldn't have happened unless they had gone to an RV show or dealer to gather information in search of something they might enjoy.

About The Food We Eat

The health community has been telling us for decades that we need to eat more fresh fruits and vegetables. The Blue Zone Studies found that eating a mostly plant-based diet was a common trait among the people who live the longest, healthiest lives on earth. A study published in the British Medical Journal that followed 65,000 people for eight years found that eating seven servings of fruit and vegetables a day will:

- Cut your risk of stroke by 25%
- Cut your risk of Heart Attack by 31%
- Lower your overall risk of death by 42%

In addition:

- Vegetables protect better than fruit.
- Fresh fruit and vegetables provided the best protection.
- Canned vegetables did not provide the same protection; in fact, they increased the risk of death by 17%.

Unfortunately, most canned fruit and vegetables today contain processed sugar or high fructose corn syrup, salt, artificial flavors and preservatives. Worse yet, almost all cans in the US are now lined with a plastic that contains BPH because it saves manufacturers a few cents a can. BPH is a known hormone disruptor that has been linked to cancer. Eden Organics is the only food manufacturer we found that refuses to use cans made with BPH. Sure, safe healthy food usually costs a little more, but how much does getting cancer cost?

Did you Know?

Study: Meat Plays a Major Role in Cancer Rates

A study published in the journal *Nutrients* analyzed

how often 21 types of cancers occurred in 87 countries with reliable cancer data and found that the majority of cancers in the world are linked to three activities: smoking, drinking alcohol and eating meat.

Study: Group Walking has Medical and Social Benefits

A study done by the University of East Anglia and published in the *British Journal of Sports Medicine* found that walking with a group can reduce the risk of coronary heart disease, depression, stroke and other life-threatening conditions.

Study: It's Easier to Develop a Healthier Habit with Your Partner

A study done by the University College in London and published in the medical journal JAMA, looked at 3,700 couples over age 50 and found couples were more likely to quit smoking, take up exercising, lose weight or improve their diet, if they worked on it together compared to trying to accomplish it alone.

Study: Incidental Exercise can Save Lives and Money

A Melbourne Australia study found that people who got "incidental" exercise by walking or biking to where they needed to go were less likely to succumb to disease or suffer premature death. Also noted was that The World Health Organization said in 2012 that just 30 minutes of daily exercise reduces the chance of premature death by 20-22%.

Study: Older Amateur Bike Riders were Younger Physically and Mentally

A King's College of London study published in the Journal of Physiology Scientists, found that regular bike riders aged 55 to 79 were biologically and physically younger than their peers who did not pedal. The were found to have better bone strength, heart, hormonal functions, lung function, metabolic rate, muscle function, neuromuscular function, oxygen intake and better reflexes. The also enjoyed better mental ability, overall health and well-being.

Study: Yoga May Be as Beneficial Health-wise as Cycling

A study published in the European Journal Of Preventive Cardiology that reviewed 37 clinical trials, showed that blood pressure fell, LDL or "bad" cholesterol dropped, "good" cholesterol increased, average heart rate lowered, and weight loss increased in subjects that practiced yoga. It was also noted that yoga may be easier for older adults to perform than many aerobic exercises.

Study: Running may Reverse Aging

Researchers from the University of Colorado and Humboldt State University in California found that running or possibly any daily strenuous activity could shave decades off your body's biological age. The great news is that you can probably benefit by starting at any age, as many involved in this study didn't begin running until they were in their 60s.

Study: Walking in a Group Through Nature Improves Mental Health

It's well known that walking through nature with others promotes physical and social activity and interaction with nature. But a new study from the University of Michigan published in the journal *Ecopsychology* found it also boosts creativity, significantly lowers depression, reduces stress and improves overall mental health and well-being.

Study: Volunteering Has Health Benefits

A study by the UnitedHealth Group and the Optimum Institute found that volunteers benefited emotionally, mentally, physically and in other ways from their good deeds. Here's just some of the benefits they reported: 49% said it helped their careers, 78% reported lower stress, 94% reported improved moods, and 96% said that volunteering increased their sense of life's purpose.

Study: Poor Sleep May be a Better Indicator of Suicide Risk in Older Adults Than Depression

Actor Robin Williams was in his 60s when he committed suicide. Many people don't realize that older adults have higher rates of suicide than other age groups. Rebecca Bernert, PhD, director of the Suicide Prevention Research Laboratory at Stanford, found that poor sleep could be a stand-alone risk factor. Suicide is preventable, and sleepiness is highly treatable.

Study: Aluminum Linked to Alzheimer's Disease and Osteoporosis

Aluminum exposure from common household products such as cookware, deodorant and tin foil has been known for some time. A study published in the International Journal of Electrochemical Science has again found aluminum to be linked Alzheimer's Disease and Osteoporosis. To avoid exposure, use glass bake and cookware and avoid using aluminum foil or antacids and deodorants that list "aluminum hydroxide" as an ingredient.

Choosing Your Best Retirement Lifestyle Option

Learning What will Really Make You Happy

The key to experiencing the best possible retirement is to learn what is really important to you and what you truly desire. That may seem obvious, but many people think they want one thing, when in reality they really want something else.

Everyone who has done the following exercise learned something about themselves that led to better lifestyle decisions. Some people were shocked at some of their own answers. You may discover that if you moved far away on a full-time basis, you'll likely miss your kids and grand-kids more than you realized before giving it serious thought. You may learn that deep down, there are a lot of places in the world you really would love to see, once you started to think about it.

Many people have never have written their thoughts and feelings down on paper before. But the simple act of thinking about a question and writing what pops into our head could help us make the best possible retirement lifestyle decisions. We may discover something about ourselves that we never realized before. We'll likely learn what will really make us happy. It will take only a few minutes, and the answers could mean the difference between enjoying an exciting adventure filled retirement and years of disappointment, boredom and even depression.

If you're like most people, you've put up with a lot to get to this point in your life. So why not entertain yourself for a few minutes with an exercise (even if you think it's silly) that may pay big dividends compared to the time invested?

Tips for getting the most out of this questionnaire:

1. Don't over-think your answers. Just write down the first answer(s) that may pop into your mind as quickly as you can. You want to write down everything the intuitive, creative part of your brain comes up with before the analytical part of your brain intrudes. You'll analyze your answers later.

2. Don't worry about neatness.

3. Be honest with yourself and just quickly write down how you really feel, no matter what it is, because that's how you really feel.

4. Remember how in the past, teachers said there

were no stupid questions? Well you're old enough to know there really are, but there are no stupid or wrong answers to these questions because it's just how you really feel.

5. Write your answers down. You won't be able to read them later if you don't write them down.

6. Don't worry about correct spelling, grammar or penmanship (as long as YOU can read it). Don't let the analytical part of your brain interfere with your creative thoughts. Just transfer your thoughts to paper as quickly as you can.

7. Your answers can be as short or long as you want, as long as you know what you mean. Just write it down and write it down quickly.

8. If you find that that the analytical, practical side of your brain starts to interfere with your creative thoughts, take a break and come back to it after 10 minutes.

9. Some people may be able to concentrate for only five minutes at a time before the practical part of the brain tries to edit. In this case, answer questions for only five minutes at a time and then take a break.

If you want to permanently move long distance for full time living:

1. What are my reasons for wanting to move?
2. What is the *main* reason?
3. What do I *hate* about where I now live?
4. What will I miss if I move away?
5. How do the other people in my life feel about me moving?

6. Could moving have a negative impact on anyone I care about?
7. Are there any family or social events that I will miss out on if I move away?
8. What holidays, graduations, weddings, reunions or other events will I travel back for?
9. How will I feel if for some reason, I can't make it to those events?
10. What holidays, events or occasions am I OK with missing out on?
11. Will I have to sell a home to move? If so, how much that will cost me?
12. Will I be moving furnishings with me? If so, how much will that cost?
13. Is my significant other really on board with moving?

What do I really want to do in retirement?

- What places in the world do I really want to see, now that I have the time?
- Is there anything special that I really would like to accomplish, like learn a new skill or language?
- If money were no object, what would I most like to be doing this very minute?
- What about tomorrow and next week?
- Would I be OK with watching many hours of TV every day becoming my main retirement activity?
- Do I feel I deserve to do what I want in retirement??

- Would I like to be healthier and in better shape, perhaps even thinner?
- Do I think an activity that is both healthy and fun should become a part of your retirement?
- Would I like excitement and adventure to be part of my retirement?
- Is there something I always wanted to do, but never had the time or chance?
- Is it possible that something I think is "stupid" might just turn out to be something I enjoy if I actually tried it?
- Would I like to be wealthier?
- Should a pursuit that is fun and puts money in my pocket be part of my retirement?
- If money weren't an object, would I like to travel? If so, where to?
- If money were no object, would I like to own more than one home or "snowbird"?
- If money were no object, would traveling to adventurous places in an RV be appealing?

Retirement Lifestyle

- Does the idea of "snowbirding" appeal to me?
- Should I give snow sports such as skiing a try?
- Does overseas travel or living appeal to me?
- Do I prefer the beach or mountains? Would the beach in winter and the mountains in summer be the way to go?
- Would full-time RVing be something I'd enjoy?

Take a few days if need be, until you feel you've

adequately answered the questions. Analyze your answers and share them with your significant other, if you have one. Then answer the last question.

- Of all of the retirement options you thought of or read about, if money were no object, what retirement option appeals the most to you?

It All Comes Down to This:

Write down your retirement plan and just start having fun!

Resources

www.BestPlaceToLiveRetire.com

This is where you can find all resource links to outside websites. If those links change or stop working, I'll find another equally valuable resource link to replace it. This way you won't end up with a book full of links that don't work.

www.StateofFloridaLiving.com

If you are thinking about moving to Florida, please visit my Florida specific blog. You also may find my book on Florida, the "Florida Move Guide" helpful.

www.RonStack.com

My team can find a top real estate broker to help you sell your home anywhere in the US. My finder service is free to you.

Alphabetical Index

Made in the USA
Lexington, KY
12 February 2017